Coping with Parental Death

EMPOWERING YOU

The Rowman & Littlefield *Empowering You* series is aimed to help you, as a young adult, deal with important topics that you, your friends, or family might be facing. Whether you are looking for answers about certain illnesses, social issues, or personal problems, the books in this series provide you with the most up-to-date information. Throughout each book you will also find stories from other teenagers to provide personal perspectives on the subject.

Coping with Parental Death

Insights and Tips for Teenagers

Michelle Shreeve

ROWMAN & LITTLEFIELD
Lanham • Boulder • New York • London

Published by Rowman & Littlefield
An imprint of The Rowman & Littlefield Publishing Group, Inc.
4501 Forbes Boulevard, Suite 200, Lanham, Maryland 20706
www.rowman.com

86-90 Paul Street, London EC2A 4NE, United Kingdom

British Library Cataloguing in Publication Information Available

Library of Congress Cataloging-in-Publication Data

Names: Shreeve, Michelle, 1984– author.
Title: Coping with parental death : insights and tips for teenagers /
   Michelle Shreeve.
Description: Lanham : Rowman & Littlefield, [2022] | Series: Empowering you
   | Includes bibliographical references and index. | Summary: "Losing a
   parent at any time in one's life is difficult, but losing a parent when
   a teenager brings its own distinct challenges. Coping with Parental
   Death offers coping strategies, expert advice, useful resources, and
   valuable insight from other young adults, providing support to those
   struggling with the death of one or both of their parents"—Provided by
   publisher.
Identifiers: LCCN 2021056031 (print) | LCCN 2021056032 (ebook) | ISBN
   9781538154892 (paperback ; alk. paper) | ISBN 9781538154908 (epub)
Subjects: LCSH: Teenagers and death. | Parents—Death—Psychological
   aspects. | Bereavement--Psychological aspects.
Classification: LCC BF724.3.D43 S467 2022 (print) | LCC BF724.3.D43
   (ebook) | DDC 155.9/370835—dc23/eng/20211221
LC record available at https://lccn.loc.gov/2021056031
LC ebook record available at https://lccn.loc.gov/2021056032

To God, Chris, and Johnny.
Thank you for piecing back together my broken heart.
I love you three more than you will ever know.

Contents

Acknowledgments

$\mathcal{I}$would like to thank God, Chris, Johnny, Kathy, Dave, Mike, Trish, Jim Gigliotti, Wendy Gigliotti, Christine Gigliotti, Ed Gigliotti, Carmela Gigliotti, Chris Putman, Vicky Camacho, Ron Camacho, Andrea Laneri-Martin, Melissa Fortune, Alicia Mooney, Jon Weeks, Kathy Esquivel, Aimee Erickson, Dr. David Schonfeld, Cara Belvin, Samantha Loutzenhiser, Empowering Her organization, Hope Edelman, Tony Ramseyer, Cody Jenkins, The Dougy Center, Christen Karniski, Erinn Slanina, Brad Meltzer, Donna Schuurman, Paul Maryniak, Times New Media, *Ahwatukee Foothills* newspaper, *Gilbert Sun News*, *San Tan Valley Sun*, *East Valley Tribune*, *The Mesa Tribune*, *The Chandler Arizonan*, Mindfulness and Grief, Southern New Hampshire University, Rebecca LeBoeuf, Pamme Boutselis, Dr. Marlen Elliot Harrison, Karla Manzella, Arlene Hirschfelder, Marsha Rafalski, Library of Congress, St. Matthews Catholic School, Mountain Pointe High School, US Census Bureau, Carl Smith, Mitch Adelson, Tami J. Suzuk, Warren Flatau, Natalie Hamilton, Chantel Dooley, PhD, Grief Haven, TAPS, COPS, the National Center for School Crisis and Bereavement, and the Coalition to Support Grieving Students for all of your help and support. All of your time and efforts helped get this book made, and I appreciate all of you. To the brave participants—Chase, Lola, Reaghan, Thad, Travis, Georgianne, Nicci, Dani R., Debbie, Liz, Sharon, Taylor, and Jessica—from the bottom of my heart, thank you for coming forward and sharing your story, for if you didn't, this book would not have been made to help others.

Welcome to the Club

If you are reading this book I know that it's because something inside of you is telling you that you have to read it. It's not like anyone wants to read a book like this. You have a piece of your heart missing, and you stumbled on this book or maybe even someone suggested it to you as you try to navigate everything you are going through. From the bottom of my heart, I am truly sorry that you are reading this book. Often people have probably told you things like "I can relate to how you feel" because they lost a loved one, but I actually truly know how you feel. You see, I lost my mother at a young age. I have been navigating the loss for the past 28 years, and I want to share everything I have learned along the way with you.

For starters, know that you have now just joined the club. The worldwide club that no teen or young adult ever wants to be a part of and doesn't willingly want to join. You joined the sadly ever-growing club of the world's youth who lost a parent young. I say club to assure you that in no way are you alone in navigating any of this. Parental death before the age of 20 is not something that anyone wants to experience. Many of your peers will never lose their parent young like you did and will never really be able to relate to what you are going through, unless they too lose a parent. Millions of children, teens, and young adults around the world, however, have lost a parent before the age of 20, so please, first and foremost, don't ever think for a second that you are alone in this. You may not know anyone personally who lost a parent young, but throughout these pages, you will learn that there are countless other teens and young adults who have experienced parental death, notable figures in society who grew up without one or both of their parents, and more who are currently navigating or who have navigated parental death before you. And remember, this worldwide club is going to be adding new members on a rolling basis. I'd like to think that you and I went through it first to help others navigate it later so we can share what we have learned along the way.

This journey is not going to be easy. It will test you in ways you will find unfair compared with your peers who still have their parents. You are going to go through a roller-coaster ride of emotions along the way, from feeling angry and envious toward your friends who still have their parents but take them for granted to mad at your parent for leaving you. Your grades might slip, your other family relationships might get rocky because everyone is on edge with their grief, and your world might be rocked because now you might have to move or switch schools since your parent passed away. To say navigating this lifelong grief you will experience from the death of your parent is a journey is an understatement. You will have hard days and good days. You will have days you think you will make your late parent proud of you and other days when you worry your late parent will be ashamed of your behavior. There will just be days. . . .

That is why I am here and why I have written this book for you. I want you to know you are not alone, and I want to prepare you as best as I can for what you are going through now and what you may experience later so you can better prepare yourself for what's to come. I would like to think I am in some way channeling all of the parents whose lives were cut short to give advice to all of the children they sadly left behind to help guide you. This experience and journey ahead will test you, change you, and can make or break you depending on what path you choose.

I hope by the end of this book you can see me as your friend from afar, someone you know in your heart can relate to what you are going through, someone who you know is always there giving you a virtual hug or even holding your hand on your hard days. I hope you find this book helpful on your good and bad days.

Let's get started, shall we?

I

UNDERSTANDING
PARENTAL DEATH

*W*hen adults go through parental death, it is often at a time that is considered a normal part of life to lose a parent. The sad reality is as we grow older through the years, so do our parents. In the normal flow of things (although sadly unique circumstances happen where this is simply not the case), children are supposed to bury their parents when the children are adults and the parents are at what is considered an elderly age. The average age for a child to lose a parent is after the child is 40 or 50 and after the parent is 60 or 70. This is not the case for all of you reading this book however. You are reading this book because you have lost your parent well younger than the average age most of your peers will lose their parent someday. Your time was significantly cut short, and you weren't even quite out of your childhood or young adult years for the time your parent was still trying to teach you lessons about life, help you fill out college applications, or to see you get ready for your prom. For some of you, your time was cut even shorter than that, and your parent wasn't there for your transition from middle school to high school, to talk to you about the birds and the bees, or to see you make the football team freshman year in high school. Chances are, you were still quite dependent on your parent emotionally, physically, financially, psychologically, and mentally when he or she passed away.

So this book is written just for you, the ones who lost a parent well before the average time they should have. Parental death to the world has a different meaning than it does for you. Parental death for you poses many upcoming challenges and hard days ahead than compared with those who lose parents after they are no longer dependent on them anymore or are at least full grown adults well into their 30s, 40s, and

1

50s. Parental death means something significantly different for you, so parental death at a young age should not be compared with parental death at an older age because it is not a fair comparison. There are so many complicated factors and variables in between the time frame that you lost your parent and others who lose their parent at an older, more average time to lose them.

Losing a parent young impacts the rest of your life in ways your peers will never experience. It forces you to see life differently, to live each moment more carefully, and to know to never take your loved ones for granted. The death of your parent affects your past, your present, and your future. We see this in the Marvel Cinematic Universe's (MCU) show, *WandaVision* for example. When Wanda Maximoff took over the town of Westview, New Jersey, everyone thought she did so because she was grieving the loss of the love of her life, Vision. In the MCU's mini-television series, we learn after just the first episodes that Wanda's grief goes well beyond just losing the love of her life, and might I add losing the love of her life right in front of her. Fans for a moment fell in love with Wanda and Vision's love story while watching the nostalgic intertwining of fan favorite television show spin-offs like the *Dick Van Dyke* show, the *Brady Bunch*, and *Bewitched* to name a few. About three episodes into the miniseries MCU fans were reminded that not only did Wanda create this new world where the love of her life still lived because she was grieving his loss but that she also was grieving the loss of her twin brother Pietro who died in close proximity to her because of Ultron. Additionally, she was grieving the loss of both of her parents, who were killed not more than several feet away from Wanda when she was a child when an explosion went off in their childhood home. Wanda's first loss that connects all of her other losses stems back to her parents' death as a child.

Wanda Maximoff is a fictional character who has gone through more than most, and she basically suffered a triple grief blow of the four most important people to her. Although taking over the town of Westview and controlling the minds of innocent people to partake in her fantasy was probably not the healthiest way to grieve her losses, she found a way that worked for her, even if only for a moment. As the miniseries unfolds, she starts to realize that she can't grieve like this forever, and not only do triggers from characters throughout the show help her start to deal and cope with the losses of her past, but she also learns a lot about herself and how truly strong of a person she is. That strength she discovers leads her to again do something hard for her to do: shut down the fantasy world she created where the love of her life still lives and go back to reality and face what she has done.

The little details the creators of the series added throughout each episode connect with how the world grieves in many ways. In Wanda's mind, her life was like the *Dick Van Dyke* show because it was the show she used to watch with her parents alongside her twin brother and the show she watched as the explosion hit her childhood home and took her parents away. She pulled pieces of her past, the happy moments, and intertwined them with the painful losses, and that is how she was trying to navigate through her grief and cope with all of the losses she had experienced.

This is how we grieve the death of our parent. Everyone grieves in a way that works best for them. We pull happy memories and find the connecting points where pain meets love and love meets pain as they both are a part of the grieving process. You will think of happy memories that you shared with your late parent and then be reminded of the pain of losing them, and that is how you too will work on navigating through your grief journey. Triggers will happen along the way—someone will say something, you will smell the same cologne your dad used to wear, or someone will laugh in a similar way your mom used to laugh, and suddenly the loss will hit you all over again, just like what happened for Wanda Maximoff. This journey you are now on will never end. You will have hard days and good days, and sad days and happy days. You just embarked on a lifelong roller-coaster ride, a ride you probably wish you didn't have to take. But that is why I am here. I am here to help you strap in safely on that ride and help prepare you as best I can for what is going on, what is to come, and to provide you with healthy coping mechanisms. Like Wanda Maximoff, you are not alone. Between the fiction and nonfiction world, you have more company than you think.

To properly understand parental death at a young age, we forge ahead keeping a quote from *WandaVision* in the back of our mind: "What is grief, if not love persevering?"

The Facts

$\mathcal{G}$oing through something difficult such as losing your parent at a young age can be challenging to navigate, especially if you feel like you're all alone. In many ways it feels like you're the only one experiencing it because you may not know someone in your community who also lost a parent before the age of 20, but there are actually millions of children, teens, and young adults who lost a parent young like you spread across the decades and across the globe. You may not know anyone in your community personally, but chances are, there are several students in your school alone who also lost a parent. There are probably parentless teens at the summer camp you attended, you just didn't know you had that in common with them. If you think you're alone, I promise you, you're not. Just check out these statistics that reflect worldwide known occasions where children, teens, and young adults lost a parent young due to a variety of different causes. This list is a hard one to read, but it is based on the facts of disastrous events that stole time between parents and their children.

- More than 500,000 children lost their father in World War I.[1]
- In World War II alone, government records show that 183,000 children lost their fathers during their service overseas.[2]
- Approximately 25,000 children have lost an active duty parent in the military over the last 35 years.[3]
- A total of 21 children lost a parent or father to the Deepwater Horizon disaster.[4]
- An estimated 13.4 million children and adolescents (0–17 years) worldwide had lost one or both parents to AIDS as of 2015.[5]

- Worldwide, an estimated 153 million children and adolescents, between newborns and 18 years old, have lost one or both of their parents, and daily, 5,760 more children lose at least one parent. It was projected that there will be around 500 million orphaned children all around the world by the end of 2018.[6]
- According to the Ministry of Health, Labor, and Welfare, as of March 2019, there were 1,554 children younger than age 18 at the time of the March 2011 Japan earthquake and tsunami who lost one parent in the disaster and 243 children lost both.[7]
- According to *Families after the Holocaust,* "Of the estimated 150,000 child survivors of the Holocaust, the majority spent at least part of the war in hiding, often separated from their families for months or even years. Some of these child survivors—an unknown number—managed to locate surviving parents at the war's end."[8]
- In the United States, each year, between 7,000 and 12,000 children lose a parent to suicide, researchers estimate.[9]
- A total of 1.5 million children globally lost a parent or caregiver from coronavirus disease in 2019 (COVID-19).[10]
- From the Oklahoma City bombing on April 19, 1995, 30 children were orphaned. A total of 219 children lost a parent.[11]
- In Haiti, Quake's Orphans Long for a Home UNICEF estimates that more than 20,000 children lost their parents in the January 12, 2010, quake and its aftermath.[12]
- The United Nations Children's Fund reported on its website that even before the magnitude 7.0 earthquake, Haiti, one of the world's poorest countries, was awash in orphans, with 380,000 children living in orphanages or group homes.[13]
- A total of 30 percent of all new military survivors connecting with Tragedy Assistance Program for Survivors (TAPS) are grieving the death of their parent; 25 percent of all new survivors connecting with TAPS in 2021 are children (younger than age 18); and 63 percent of all new children (younger than age 18) connecting with TAPS in 2021 are grieving the death of their father.[14]

These statistics show that clearly you're not the only one who has lost a parent in history. However, reading these statistics isn't going to make you feel any better because these statistics aren't going to bring your parent back. These statistics should prove to you that you are indeed not alone in this grief journey and that there are millions out there in the world that in many ways can actually relate to parts of what you're going through. Sadly the list of statistics goes on and on far beyond this small sampling of a list where children, teens, and young adults lost a parent before the age of 20.

As you continue reading this book, I'll provide you with coping mechanisms that can help you on your especially hard grief trigger days. However, take these statistics and let them encourage you to reach out to other parentless teens and young adults. If you don't know anyone at your school who lost a parent like you did, why not start a club? You never know how many other teens or young adults lost a parent, and by starting a club, you can help other teens and young adults not feel alone like maybe you do. Looking at these statistics pertaining to children, teens, and young adults who lost a parent in the line of law enforcement or firefighter duty or during active military duty, why not reach out to the countless organizations out there that focus on grieving families who lost a parent in the military such as the Tragedy Assistance Program for Survivors (TAPS) organization, or if your late parent was a fallen police officer, reach out to the Concerns of Police Survivors (COPS) organization, or a fallen firefighter, reach out to the National Fallen Firefighters Foundation. Some of these organizations host grief camps or support group meetings where teens and young adults like you can meet others who lost a parent, too. They might additionally offer resources or host workshops and can provide you and your family helpful support. Check out the resources section at the end of this book for a list of organizations that can help.

• 2 •

Types of Death

$\mathcal{T}$eens and young adults have lost one or both of their parents like you have from a wide range of causes. Some parents have died from an accident, an illness, suicide, crime, natural disasters, and other reasons. Perhaps your late parent died from one of these causes. Losing a parent is a difficult life event to experience especially because you are so young, but the type of death as well as other extenuating circumstances, such as expected or unexpected, sudden deaths, or more can complicate your grief as well. Let's go over the most common types of parental deaths to see which category your late parent falls in. These are the most common, but there are additional ways teens and young adults have lost a parent.

ACCIDENTS

Accidents can be categorized under the unexpected death in which case no one knew an accident was going to take your parent away. Whether a car accident, a boating accident, a plane accident, or other situational accidents that can occur, an accident is usually a sudden and unexpected type of death. This means you did not see your parent's death coming and had no time to prepare.

ILLNESS

This type of death is common for teens to lose one or both of their parents to. An illness usually gives you time to prepare for your parent's upcoming death. Nothing can truly ever prepare you for the death of your parent, but when a parent is battling an illness, it may have presented you with a little time. Your parent might have been undergoing cancer treatments, or was battling AIDS, COVID-19, or a heart condition. How you are dealing with your grief from the death of your parent will depend on the illness. If your parent was battling cancer for a few years and had several cancer treatments since diagnosis, you may have had time to psychologically prepare for their death. If you lost a parent during the current COVID-19 pandemic we are experiencing, then your grief will have more complicated extenuating circumstances because the pandemic is ongoing. It will also complicate your grief, especially if you weren't allowed to visit your parent in the hospital if they had COVID-19. Again, every teen and young adult's story of parental death is different, and although these types of deaths are the most common to categorize, not every parental death is the same.

THE STORIES OF THOSE
WHO LOST A PARENT TO AN ILLNESS

I lost my mother when I was 15 years old. My mom was 49 when she died of breast cancer.—Thad[1]

My mum passed away from cervical cancer. But my dad has said that it was most possibly the morphine and chemo that killed her (2004–2005 technology obviously wasn't as advanced).—Jessica[2]

[I lost my father to] colon cancer. He had many rounds of surgeries, chemo and radiation over the years. He even went into remission a few times. But it relentlessly returned.—Liz[3]

I was 14 years old when [my mother] passed away from cervical cancer. She had been sick for a while. She had been given the cancer diagnosis about two and a half years earlier and was quite sick while going through treatments.—Travis[4]

My mother passed away from non-Hodgkin Lymphoma. My mom had been sick off and on for almost three years.—Dani R.[5]

I was 17 when I lost my father. He passed away from cardiac arrest at work. He had struggled with heart problems since 2015 and has had countless heart attacks.—Reaghan[6]

My father died from complications of a rare blood disorder. It is called catastrophic antiphospholipid syndrome. Antiphospholipid syndrome is more common, though not terribly common itself. However, in 2010, when my father developed catastrophic antiphospholipid syndrome, there were only 300 known cases on the planet that had occurred in the present and past. Fifty percent of those cases never made it out of the hospital. Most of them had co-occurring conditions at diagnosis such as lupus, rheumatoid arthritis, or Sjögren syndrome. My dad had none; he was a healthy 51 year old at the time he fell ill, with no known risk factors at the time of falling ill. We did not have an autopsy performed (not my choice) but my assumption has always been that he had something that needed surgically repaired that had become septic and that is what actually killed him, but because doctors were trying to manage the condition it was overlooked.—Sharon[7]

My Personal Story

In the 1980s, the doctors advised my mother to get a blood transfusion. Although my mother hesitated, she ultimately agreed to getting one. My mother ended up getting an HIV-infected blood transfusion, which led to her contracting AIDS. My mother ended up passing away from AIDS-related pneumonia in 1993.

At the time of her sickness and leading up to her death, we lived in the Bay Area in California, one of the focus areas where HIV and AIDS were controversial topics around the community. A lot of people, doctors, and members of the community did not know how to react to those living with AIDS at the time. Due to this, my family thought it would be best if no one knew the truth about how my mother died, as a way to protect my brother and I at school. Looking back now, almost 30 years since my mother's death, I understand the decision to keep the cause of her death quiet, but internalizing how she died instead of opening up to close friends, family members, and school and community members, in my opinion, complicated mine and my family's grief in many different ways throughout all of these years.

As you are learning, it is not easy to open up and talk about the death of your parent. Through time you will find it healing to open up to the right people about your parent's death. Over the years, I wanted to open up to many of my friends and other family members about how my mother died, but I was always too afraid to. I thought that if I shared the truth I would either get in trouble with my family for not keeping her death private, or that sharing would cause my family trouble for how the world around us would react. I was afraid of what people might think or say or afraid of disappointing my family members by sharing and not keeping it private. Again, I understand why they wanted to keep quiet about the situation because the world and our community was reacting to the disease in lots of mostly negative ways at the time, but holding in how she died after almost three decades, in my opinion, has delayed and complicated the grieving process even more.

Looking back, I often think how life would be different and if I would have healed in a more positive way had I been able to tell others freely how she really died. I also think about how my mother must have been feeling during the final months of her death. Because no one really knew what she had or what she was dying from, did she feel lonely? Did she want to tell one of her friends or a neighbor but was too afraid of how they would react? I feel bad for thinking my mother felt alone toward the end and for how maybe she had the desire to want to have told someone but feeling like maybe she couldn't. Maybe she was trying to protect us as she was dying, but I never would have wanted my mother to die feeling all alone. If she told friends or neighbors, maybe she could have had more support toward the end.

Keeping the truth about how your parent died a secret might be something you are dealing with silently as well. Maybe your family has asked you not to reveal the truth about how your parent died for a number of reasons. Whatever the reason might be, know that it can complicate your grief in the long run by not sharing the truth to those closest to you about how your parent died. If your family is asking to keep the cause of your parent's death a secret, I strongly suggest talking to your family members about at least being able to open up to one person about it. It can do more damage than good in the long run regarding your coping journey than your family may realize all to just hide the truth from others.

SUICIDE

Suicide is an unexpected parental type of death. You were most likely blindsided by this type of death and perhaps you didn't even know that your late parent was contemplating suicide or was thinking suicidal thoughts. This type of parental death also brings feelings of guilt for the surviving family members because you might blame yourself for not seeing the signs or regret saying or not saying something that could have potentially (in your mind) changed your late parent's mind to die by suicide. There are also so many unanswered questions you might have for your late parent and why they chose to end their life. If you are having a hard time with navigating your parent's death to suicide, reach out to a trusted adult as soon as possible for support.

CRIME

This is also another form of an unexpected type of parental death. Maybe your late parent was just going to work, and they were robbed and killed in the parking garage. Or perhaps your late parent was shopping at a store and a shooting broke out that ended your late parent's life. Losing your parent to a crime can evoke feelings of anger and rage toward the person responsible for the crime that led to the death of your parent. Again, you didn't see their death coming, and now due to someone else's actions, your parent is not here anymore.

TERRORIST ATTACKS

Unfortunately, attacks against innocent people can happen that can take lives, including the lives of parents and forcing a premature separation from their children. An example of this are the September 11, 2001, attacks where 3,000 children lost a parent in a single day. This horrific and heartbreaking event sparked global collective grief in which grief was experienced in a large community wave that affected millions of people around the world. Not everyone lost someone that day or lost a parent, but many were grieving the lives lost and all that happened on this day.

NATURAL DISASTERS

This can also be seen as another type of unexpected parental death. With everything in the news lately that you hear about the hurricanes, tornadoes, tsunamis, and earthquakes, many children have lost a parent due to natural disasters. There might be warning systems in place that have tried to help families prepare and escape a natural disaster, but that doesn't mean anyone is immune from being killed by a natural disaster, and this includes parents.

MOVIE BREAK: *TWISTER*

In the movie, Jo lost her father during a deadly F-5 tornado when she was just a little girl. The loss of her father at a young age due to a tornado fueled Jo and led her down a path to study tornadoes as she grew up. She strongly felt that there could be a better advanced warning system so that families wouldn't have to lose loved ones to tornadoes like she lost her father. She ended up building a machine that detects the danger level of a tornado while also meeting and working with the love of her life. She had a few close calls while trying to get her machine to work, but her hard work paid off and she was successfully able to detect tornadoes and their strength. She just wished the machine could have been built so her dad hadn't died when she was little, but at least now in the future, fathers wouldn't be separated from their daughters with the new warning system in place.[8]

IN THE LINE OF DUTY: LAW ENFORCEMENT, FIREFIGHTERS, AND ARMED FORCES

Many parents bravely and courageously protect communities, towns, cities, and countries from outside threats in exchange for putting their lives on the line. Unfortunately, lives can be lost in professions such as being a firefighter, a police officer, or serving in the armed forces. There are many children who have lost one or both of their parents who were fighting a fire, protecting the community, or serving in the Army or in the Navy.

DRUG ADDICTION OR SUBSTANCE ABUSE

As we face an opioid crisis, it just brings to the surface that many adults struggle with drug addiction or substance abuse. Although some might be getting help or attending rehab, some might be falling through the cracks or may not be at the point where they realize or admit they are struggling with an addiction. Others may know they have an addiction that is not healthy for them, but they might not know how to stop it or don't want to stop. This is a situation in which a lot of children around the world have lost one or both of their parents.

You might not know any other teen or young adult who lost a parent at all, let alone in the same way that you lost yours, but there are countless organizations out there that can help point you in the right direction to meet other teens and young adults who lost their parent in a similar way. Connecting with others that are your age who lost a parent can provide you more support while you are navigating your parental death journey. Finding others who lost a parent in the same way you did can only benefit you even more to not feel alone with what you are going through.

No matter how your parent died, their death is going to leave a hole in your heart—a void that you will long to fill. Nothing will ever be able to replace your late parent or the love they had for you, but read on to find ways that can help you live your best and healthy life despite now having to finish growing up without your parent physically being there for you.

• 3 •

How Life Changes

*L*ife after a parental death can significantly change well after the funeral. Your life was going one way, and then suddenly with your late parent absent now, lots of things are going to change. Your surviving parent or caregiver will probably try and keep everything the same for you as best as they can, but how can things be the same if one important person is suddenly missing from your life? Losing your parent can expose you to what are called secondary losses.

WHAT ARE SECONDARY LOSSES?

Secondary losses are losses you might be experiencing that are directly related from the death of your parent. For example, if your father died and he was the sole provider to your family, your family might now have to make financial cutbacks. You might not be able to do extracurricular activities after school because your family can't afford it. Or if your mother died, and your father was never in the picture, you might have to move in with another relative. And that relative can be in another state, so now you are not just having to deal with the death of your parent, which is tragic enough, but on top of that, you also have to deal with the stress of moving to a new state, starting at a new school, and having to make new friends. These are secondary losses that were caused in relation to the death of your parent. In other words, you most likely would not be going through these losses and changes had your parent not died. Losses of routine, finances, stability, friends, your room—these are all secondary losses.

Let's go more in depth of the different types of secondary losses there are and ideas for how to help navigate these new changes that you might be going through.

NEW HOME

Let's say you lived with your late mother. Now that she passed away, if it was just the two of you, you now have to move in with another family member because you can't live in your home alone. So the home you once knew that reminded you of your late mother and all the memories you made together is something you have to leave even though that would help comfort you during this time to stay there because it's familiar. On top of that, now you have to pack up your stuff, potentially donate some of your mother's items, and move somewhere new. That's tough. That's a lot to deal with, especially while you're still mourning the loss of your mom. To help with the transition, ask your new guardian if maybe you can place some items from your home around your new home that remind you of your mother. Maybe your mom's desk where she did crafts can go into your new room. Maybe your mom's favorite kitchen decorative picture can go in your new kitchen, too. Even if your new home has plenty of blankets, maybe your guardian will let you bring over the blankets that you and your late mother picked out together. Talk to your guardian about what can help you with this transition.

FOSTER CARE

If you lost both of your parents and don't have any other relatives or family friends to come and take over caring for you, you might have been placed in foster care. While in foster care, you can be adopted and placed in a permanent home. Going to foster care after losing your parents can be a challenging transition. It is important to talk to a trusted adult or counselor about how you are feeling and expressing what your needs are during this difficult time because there are several new and potentially uncomfortable and stressful changes taking place.

NEW SCHOOL

Let's say you lived with your late father because your mother and father were separated. Now that your father is no longer here, you have to move in with your mother who lives in another state. That means you will have to attend a new school. This can be tough because it means new teachers, new routines, new friends to make, perhaps you have to give up being on the baseball team, and more. To help with this transition, talk to your guardian to see if you can join the baseball team at your new school, go with them to pick out your new school so you're involved in the process, see if you can join similar clubs, or see if the new school has a program to partner you up with a peer to help you learn about the new school, meet new students, teachers, and more.

NEW ROUTINES

If your mother was the one you spent the majority of your time with, who helped you get ready for school and took you to sports games and friends' houses, then all of this will change because it switches to your surviving father now taking on these roles. This means new routines will probably be put into place because your dad might do things differently than your late mother did. He might try to keep things the same as possible, but since your mom and dad are two different individuals, routines are going to be a new normal for you. Maybe your dad is new to cooking, so dinner might taste and look different now. Due to your dad's work schedule, he might need you to carpool with one of your peers to soccer practice instead of him driving you like your mother used to do. You might have to wake up earlier now for school for your dad to drop you off before he has to go to work. To help with this transition, keep communication lines open with your dad. It's okay to tell him how you and your mom used to do routines, but be kind and patient and realize that your dad is learning new roles while also trying to balance the new loss of his wife, your mother. If something as a part of the new routines isn't working for you, talk to your dad so you guys can work together to try and come up with something that can work for the both of you.

NEW RESPONSIBILITIES

Maybe you're the oldest of four children your parents had and your late dad worked from home and used to be the one to get you all up in the morning and ready for school. Now that your dad is gone, your mother is juggling suddenly being a single mom of four and working to put food on the table and keep a roof over all of your heads. Chances are, because you're the oldest, she might need your help waking up your younger siblings. She might also need you guys all to pitch in and help with chores such as dishes or laundry, something you might not be used to doing. To help with this transition, appreciate that she's asking you for help because that shows she knows you are responsible enough to help. Although it might be hard and might cause you to give up your free time, know that your late dad would be proud that you are stepping up to help. If you are struggling with the new responsibilities, talk to your mom and maybe you guys can work out a time where once a week you get free time to yourself to give you a mental break.

MOVIE BREAK: *27 DRESSES*

In the movie, Jane and Tess lose their mother at a young age. As now a widower and single parent to young girls, their grieving father struggles with the day to day life of taking care of two little girls by himself. Jane, the oldest, recognizes that her father is struggling ever since their mother died and maturely steps in. Although Jane was young and grieving too, because she was the oldest, she stepped into a caretaker role while growing up with her sister for both her younger sister and her father.[1]

NEW LIFESTYLE

When your dad was alive, both of your parents were maybe working, and you were able to get the newest clothes, go on a few vacations each year, and perhaps even earned a weekly allowance. Now that your dad is suddenly gone, if he was the breadwinner, things could drastically change for you and your siblings. Now you are a family that lives off of one income, which means your mom might have to make cuts to make ends meet. You now might only be able to go on one vacation a year if any at all, you might not be able to buy new clothes as often as you are used to, and you might not be able to get an allowance anymore. To help with this transition, be open to communication with your mom. Maybe tell her what cuts are hard for you or mention the ones that bother you and maybe you guys can work something out such as cutting from another category that's more okay with you, or maybe you can talk about getting a part-time job to pay for the clothes you want.

NEW STEPPARENT OR NEW SURVIVING PARENT ROMANTIC RELATIONSHIP

Although this one might be really hard to accept, it is not uncommon for your surviving parent to remarry or to date again after the death of your parent, their spouse. It seems unimaginable that your surviving parent would ever want to remarry, especially in a short time frame after your late parent died, but it happens. If it happens to you, definitely talk to your surviving parent and let them know how you are feeling about this new and big change. You might be on a different level of grieving your late parent than your surviving parent is, so you want to make sure you are being honest with how you are feeling.

ADJUSTING TO HOW LIFE CHANGED

Life changed in that we moved away from my dad's side of the family. That was extremely hard because they were a major part of our lives. Everything changed and not in a good way. My mother got involved with an abusive man, something that we had never experienced. My grades did drop because there was too much turmoil and abuse going on at home. I was just trying to survive. I did not cope with the loss or changes in a healthy way basically because I didn't know how and no one helped. We were not allowed to grieve or talk about my father's death. We just kept all feelings and sadness inside.—Georgianne[2]

I used to feel guilty for missing [my mother] because my dad had moved on and met someone new when I was five and they had married when I was 16. She was a good step-mum while I was young and impressionable, but as I developed into my own person, that's when we started to clash.—Jessica[3]

I feel like my stepfather has acted as a great role model and person to look up to.—Chase[4]

Secondary losses are hard to deal with, especially because you are trying to deal with the new life you have after your parent died. Keeping communication open with your surviving parent or new guardian is important because you want to let the adults in your life know how you feel.

My Secondary Losses

My mother died in December 1993. At the time we were living in California. After her death, my father took some time off work and was home for the first year. He would take us to school, he was the one to make our school lunches or take us clothes or grocery shopping, and he was the one who now coordinated us going to basketball practice or to a friend's house. Shortly after, my dad started dating again. In 1995, he started dating a woman named Trish. In 1996, two and a half years after my mother died, my dad married Trish and she became my stepmom. I was not ready for my dad to remarry nor was I wanting to call my stepmom "mom." So Trish moved into our home where my mother had lived, and she was the one who took us to school or took us grocery shopping or to friends' houses. In 1997, when the school year was almost over, my dad told my brother and I that when the school year ended, we would be moving to Arizona, where we didn't know

Figure 3.1. It can be stressful when your surviving parent starts dating someone new or even remarries after your parent died. That is why it is important to keep lines of communication open with your surviving parent or guardian to tell them how you are honestly feeling. Illustration by Kate Haberer

anyone. We would be living in a new home, attending a new school, dad and Trish would have new jobs, not to mention the climate change was polar opposite. I was pretty upset. In summer 1997, I was forced to leave the home I lived in with my late mother whom I was very close to, leave the area we lived in that was filled with memories of when we ate donuts with our mother before school, shopping with her at the local mall, and even leaving all of our relatives. I had to leave the school I was attending for eight years with all my friends when I only had two years left to complete the school, and we moved to Arizona in the summer when we didn't know anyone. When school started, I began seventh grade, and I was badly bullied the whole first year I attended. The school made me and the bullies go to daily counseling so I missed a lot of class time. It was a stressful time going through all of those changes.

So here is a quick overview of my secondary losses and new changes that I had to adjust to:

My mother died in 1993 (loss of parent).
My dad remarried in 1996 (remarriage and new stepmother).
We moved to Arizona in 1997 (new home).
I was bullied in the Arizona school from 1997 to 1998 (new school which led to bullying).

After my mother died, my secondary losses included my dad's remarriage and getting a stepmother, moving away, losing my home with my mother, starting a new school, loss of routines, loss of friends, loss of family members, and getting bullied. This all happened within five years of my mother's death, which was a lot for me to deal with as a kid. My mom died when I was nine and this is what I dealt with until I was almost 14 years old. Losing my mother was hard enough to deal with, and these extenuating secondary losses and changes complicated my grieving process even more. Looking back, I don't think I started grieving properly until I was in my mid-20s. Had I not gone through all of these secondary losses within a short amount of time after the death of my mother, maybe I could have started grieving properly sooner.

I also remember my dad told me he wanted me to go back to school right away after her death to try and keep my life as normal as possible. Going back to a school where my friends were helped a little but at the same time made it challenging for me. At the time, only one of my other peers lost a parent young like I did, so out of the whole school, only two of us lost a parent. It didn't make me feel normal going back; it actually made me suddenly feel like an outcast. Looking back, I wish my father homeschooled me. Being in a school with no one else who lost a parent like I did made me feel abnormal, and it was a distraction from me studying in school. It got worse when my dad pulled me out of that school with all my friends and put me in a new school where I got bullied. Looking back, homeschooling would have saved me from a lot of extra pain that I dealt with at a young age, and I feel I would have done better at school and concentrated better.

My dad also put me in a basketball camp a few months after my mom died because he thought that would help cheer me up by being with other kids. It was an all-girls camp about three hours away from my home and other relatives to where I didn't know anyone. I was so homesick that I used to cry myself to sleep every night at camp. The camp was two weeks long, and it was too soon for me to be separated from my family like that after my mom died. I know my dad's intentions were good, but for me, that was torture. Now there are grief camps, and I wish I was sent to a grief camp instead, where I would have been surrounded by others my age who lost a parent like I did, so I could have felt less alone.

All of these changes happened so fast that I remember feeling overwhelmed and like I never had any time to adjust to each new change properly. I remember feeling like everything was always fight or flight.

BULLYING

Unfortunately, there are teens out there who bully other teens. Perhaps the reasoning is because they do not get enough attention from their parents at home, they have a troubled life with their personal family situation, or they just think it makes them feel good and look good to others if they bully others. Whatever the case, bullying does happen. Sometimes, teens get bullied because they are different. The norm is that most teens have a mother and a father. So if suddenly you lost your mother or father, now in the eyes of your peers, you are considered different than them—and being different is often what leads to getting bullied. If you find you are suddenly getting bullied because of the death of your parent, it is imperative that you tell your surviving parent or guardian, your teacher, and your school counselor at once. Adding bullying on top of what you are dealing with can just complicate your grief even more. Please don't wait; speak up and say something right away so the bullying can stop and you can get back to your own personal grief journey again. You are going to have your hands full enough just being a teen and working through your grief. You don't need to add bullying to your plate, trust me.

There will be many life changes after your parent dies. Some changes might not be covered on this list. The important lesson to take away from this chapter is to communicate, be honest with your feelings, and reach out to trusted adults to help get you the support you need.

• 4 •

The First Year Milestones

The time leading up to your parent's death and the first year after your parent dies is hard to face because there are so many changes. Knowing what might be different during the first year after your parent dies will give you a head's up of what you can expect during this first year.

DREAMS AND NIGHTMARES

My Nightmares

Because my mother was frequently visiting the hospital toward the end, I started having nightmares. I think my mom sensed that her days were getting numbered because she used to randomly break down crying and tell me that she wanted to see me get married one day and graduate from school. Being a nine-year-old, I couldn't understand why my mom felt like she wasn't going to see me graduate or get married, so I would hug her and try and comfort her by telling her she would be there for me. I know she wasn't there in the form that she wanted to be, but in my heart, my mother was very much present for both events.

One nightmare I had was that our house caught on fire, and everyone made it out okay, except my mother. Another reoccurring nightmare I had was that my mom's favorite tea kettle overflowed and the whole house filled with water, and everyone made it outside except her. My mother, bless her for this, as she was dying was still mothering me. She would come into my room and snuggle in bed with me, hold me, and comfort me, saying everything was okay. She would stay in my bed until I fell back asleep and then she would go back to her bed. My amazing mother did this while she was sick and dying just to comfort me. I think my subconscious was in a way trying to prepare me for what was about to happen.

FIRST DAY

On the first day that you find out that your parent died, your world completely stops. Whether you found out at school, while at a friend's house, or while on vacation, it doesn't matter where you are—your heart breaks and you can't believe your parent is gone. Finding out the news brings a wave of emotions, and the day can get overwhelming with people filling your house to offer support, cooked meals, hugs, but also lots of questions arise regarding planning the funeral or related to your parent's death. While you are still trying to accept that your parent is gone forever, everyone around you is trying to make everything so fast-paced when in those moments you wish everyone would make time stand still so you can grieve.

THE DAY THAT IT HAPPENED

[The day that he died] was and continues to be the hardest day of my life. It was two weeks before I graduated high school. His breath rattled painfully as he struggled to draw in air. He hadn't spoken all day. I was sitting in my kitchen with a friend when my mom's friend came running out of the bedroom yelling, "I think your dad just died."

I fell out of my chair and started crying hysterically. It seemed like suddenly my house was filled with people. Paramedics, neighbors, friends. Apparently, I ran to my neighbor's house yelling for help, but I have no memory of doing that. My sister was at a movie with her boyfriend because we hadn't realized how close my dad was to the end. Our kind neighbors went to the theater to find her and brought her home. Activity swiveled around us for a while. My uncle came, my aunt came. My grandma came. Then, slowly everyone left. That was hard, when it was quiet again. We just had to go to bed. That first night, going to bed, waking up, it's a blur in my memory.—Liz[1]

The day my mom died, my dad came into my room and told me she was gone. Since I was the oldest (my brother was a year younger and my sister was nine), he thought I should know first. I remember a numbness coming over me and it was like my reality physically shifted in that moment. You see stuff like that in movies or TV sometimes where they make the effect with cameras.—Thad[2]

She had been in the hospital this last time, maybe a month? I can't quite remember. My grandmother and I had gone to visit her several times that week. The last time prior to her death was July 19th. It was her birthday and she turned 36 (29 for the 7th time). I had bought her this beautiful coral pajama set. She was somewhat cognizant and really liked the gift. I hugged her and told her I loved her. She had been disconnected from food and water for a few days and they were waiting for us to go before they upped her morphine. That was the last day my mom was aware of her surroundings. Two days later, July 21st, my grandmother and I had gotten there in the morning to see her. By that point she was out of it. She would mumble occasionally, but I still spoke to her. Trying really hard not to cry. We told her we would be back, since I was leaving for a bit. My grandmother and I left for maybe two hours? On our way back to the hospital my grandmother was pulled over for speeding. I remember my grandmother crying to the officer that she was in a hurry to get back to the hospital because her daughter was dying. My grandmother got the ticket and we got back to the hospital. When we arrived to her room, she was gone. They already moved her. I remember thinking, How can that be? I just saw her. It doesn't happen that fast. Did she know I loved her? Why couldn't they wait to move her? I became angry. My grandmother was distraught.—Dani R.[3]

The day I found out was February 13, 2021, at 8:10 a.m. I remember it like it was yesterday. My eldest sister got a knock on her door at 6 a.m., and it was an officer that was informing her that he was gone. My other sister and her boyfriend came out to my grandparents' house where I was spending the weekend. They woke us all up—my grandparents, my little brother who is 12, and myself. She called a family meeting and told us what had happened. The world seemed like it had stopped spinning. I have never felt such pain in my life. It felt like a part of me died with him. It didn't feel real, I felt like I was in a dream and any moment I would wake up and he would be okay. I never woke up. It was real and it was heart shattering.—Reaghan[4]

I didn't find out. . . . I was there. My mom and I had gone from Fort Wayne to Indianapolis where Dad had been transferred (for the fourth time) because it was a teaching hospital. We had gone without my younger sister who was 17 because my mom was under the impression my dad would "be fine." I had a strong gut feeling he would not be. When we got to the hospital, I asked if there was anything that could be done . . . if I could donate blood, plasma, a kidney, anything to make things change. The look on the doctor's face said it all, and he told us it was time to gather anyone important. My mom still didn't seem to grasp the gravity of the situation. She took me to the hotel we had stayed at every time we were in Indy and I had a friend who lived there come stay with me, while she went to meet my sister back at the hospital. My mom's phone lost reception in the hospital, and about an hour later I received a call. The hospital. My body went cold. I can still feel it now when I think about that moment. I picked up the phone. I said, "my mom should be there. What is going on?" They hung up. I looked at my friend, she said, "let's get in the car." I couldn't feel my legs, or the lower half of my body. I don't know how I made it to the car, I couldn't feel anything. It was dark outside; dad died after 9 p.m. Mom called and asked where I was, I managed to blurt something about being in a car. Mom said, "I'll meet you in the lobby." She met me in the lobby. We walked to the elevators we had grown so familiar with. I couldn't even tell you what floor we rode to at IU Health, but it has a big glass room in the middle of it. We arrived upstairs and my dad had just passed. I sat at his bedside and cursed, screaming at God for taking my dad from me. Someone I desperately needed. Someone I had no idea how I was going to do life without.—Sharon[5]

FIRST WEEK

During the first week after your parent dies, it gets a little overwhelming. Not only are you trying to deal with and accept the fact that your parent is now gone, but the funeral arrangement process can also get a little stressful and overwhelming. Here you are sad and thinking about your late parent, when people are bombarding you with questions like, "When is the funeral?" "Where will the funeral be?" "What music do you want to play while the casket is being brought in?" The questions will seem so tedious, not to mention how many people will be calling your house to check on you and your surviving family members, and ask questions about the funeral—not to mention the amount of people coming in and out of your house suddenly. From the time you find out your parent died, to the time the funeral is over, that first week will be an overwhelming blur of an emotional roller-coaster ride.

FIRST MONTH

When the funeral is over, everyone seems to think that you will just move on from your late parent's death and your life will get back to "normal." There is nothing normal about this time because a new normal will be forming. This is the month where those secondary losses might take shape. This is when you will notice changes that stem from the death of your parent. You will now be welcomed to the new world of before and after: how things were before your parent died to how things are now after your parent died. You might struggle with sudden fears of being separated from your surviving family members, you might

Figure 4.1. In the exact moment that you find out your parent died, so many emotions come rolling to the surface. It can be really overwhelming as you try and process the news about your parent. Illustration by Kate Haberer

have difficulty concentrating in class and potentially trying to catch up on missed classwork during the funeral week, or you might not have much of an appetite. The first month is a major adjustment month that can span many months because this is a drastic life change for you.

REAGHAN'S EXPERIENCE

Nothing helped [me] cope [at first] actually. I didn't leave my bed for days, I didn't eat. I was always nauseous and sleeping cause I was all drugged up. At first it was definitely unhealthy, but I'm getting back to normal, but I still need improvement. I've been refusing to see a counselor because it still hurts too much to talk about it. But this book can help so many understand that they aren't alone so it's worth a little heartbreak.[6]

FIRST BIRTHDAY

Celebrating your birthday with your late parent may have been a blast in the past for you, and your past birthdays were filled with fun and precious memories you had with your late parent. Don't be surprised, however, if you aren't really in the mood to celebrate your first birthday without them. It's the first year they aren't there for your birthday, so this birthday will definitely be different for you. The same goes for your parent's first birthday that they are now not here for you to celebrate.

FIRST MOTHER'S OR FATHER'S DAY

This one will sting a little, especially when your old jealousy pal (more about this in upcoming chapters) will kick in as you see your friends spend Mother's or Father's Day with their parents, and now reality sets in that your late parent will never be here again to share another one with you. Fond memories of Mother's or Father's Days of the past will surely shed you a few tears.

FIRST HOLIDAY SEASON

Whether you celebrate Kwanzaa, Christmas, Thanksgiving, and more, the first holiday season without your parent will also sting a little. The holidays are usually a time of family bonding, togetherness, and memory making, so the realization that your mom won't be there to bake her famous pumpkin pie, or your dad won't be there to carve the turkey is going to be a harsh reality check.

FIRST DEATH ANNIVERSARY

The first death anniversary marks a milestone that's challenging to navigate. While your peers just have a birthday milestone each year to signify they are one year older and one year closer to adulthood and independence, you have an additional different milestone that you will be keeping track of. The death anniversary is something in the back of your mind you will be keeping track of each year—how long your parent has been gone. The first year marks the end of the hardest year of adjustment of the fact that your parent is now gone. Each year moving forward can present different challenges, but be wise not to think that as the years go on it will get easier. Different life events can trigger the grief you feel for the death of your parent at any time. The first death anniversary is just a harsh realization that you just made it a full year without your parent.

My First Year Milestones

I remember the day we found out the news. I woke up on a Friday morning looking at my alarm clock realizing it didn't go off. I was late for school and wondering why my dad didn't wake my brother and I up. We left the hospital late the night before to visit my mom, but we had done that so many times before, what was different about this time? I walked down the hall and found my dad in the living room, just putting the phone down. I asked him how come he didn't wake us up for school. He then broke the news that my mother passed away last night, and we instantly both burst into tears. My brother came in shortly after and my dad told him what happened, too, and we all just cried.

Our house began filling up with people, and we received multiple phone calls asking about funeral arrangements or giving out condolences. I remember feeling overwhelmed. Although everyone calling or stopping by or bringing us dinners were people we knew—friends, family, neighbors, people from the school or community—we had never had that many people call us or be in our house in one day. People started going through my mother's clothes, we made visits to the church and funeral home, and suddenly the day of the funeral arrived. My mother's funeral was so packed that there was a line of people out the door.

I don't really remember the first week after the funeral, but during that first month, I remember we returned to school, and my classmates handed me a stack of handmade cards they made to try and comfort me. Although I was surrounded by all of my friends again, most who also knew my mother, I remember feeling suddenly different than all of them. Before my mother died, I was their friend. After my mother died, I was now the friend without a mother when all of my friends still had their mothers and fathers. Although my friends, classmates, and teachers tried to comfort me the best way they knew how, I suddenly felt alone even though people were surrounding me with hugs and support.

During that first year without my mother, reality sunk in when I approached the different milestones of the first birthday without her, and Mother's Day was especially hard that first year. I really felt alone because all of my friends still had their mothers, and I was literally the only one who did not. I remember feeling left out when my friends had mother-daughter sleepovers. They were kind and still tried to include me, but it wasn't the same. The first Christmas was especially hard because my mom died December 3. She had already started wrapping presents and putting them under our Christmas tree before she died, but she sadly did not make it to that 1993 Christmas to watch everyone open them. That first Christmas was a sad Christmas, and I remember it didn't have that traditional Christmas happiness and cheery disposition that the previous Christmases had when my mother was still alive. The first death anniversary was surreal. I remember my dad, brother, and I had a picnic at my mom's grave at the cemetery. We brought lunch and sat in silence on lawn chairs and shared memories as if we were having lunch with my mom.

Everyone's first year milestones will turn out different than others. Just remember to proceed in ways that are best for you and do what you need to do and focus on how you need to learn to cope in a healthy way with the death of your parent. Maybe on Mother's Day, you just want to be alone that first year to grieve the loss of your mother in your own way. Or maybe your aunt will step up, and you guys can do stuff in honor of your late mother. Or maybe you want to get together with friends and go see a movie in honor of your late father. Or perhaps you just want to stay in bed under the covers all day. All of this is okay. Just know that the first year without your parent has some milestones that can stir some different kinds of feelings for you.

· 5 ·

The Challenges

Losing a parent is going to present several challenges throughout the remainder of your childhood and beyond. Again, I am here to comfort you and prepare you in the best way I possibly can. I am also trying to provide you with helpful tools and resources to arm you for the future while you are navigating through your grief. Different feelings and emotions are likely to arise while you are suddenly trying to adjust to this new life. Let's go over a couple potential challenges for you that could happen, have already happened, or might currently be happening.

YOUR GRADES MIGHT SLIP

When your late parent was still alive, maybe you were an honor roll student, had the highest percentage in your class, or were one of the top academic performers for your grade. Don't be surprised if that changes. Losing a parent alters your reality because you just went through something devastating. You might find that you are having difficulty concentrating in class when your Literature teacher is reading a classic story that has to do with the death of a parent. You can suddenly feel overwhelmed with your classwork or even homework. Maybe your dad used to help you with your homework, and now that he's gone, your mom is busy trying to hold down the fort with you and your siblings and might not have extra time to help you with your homework like your dad used to. Your grades can slip especially during the first year after your parent died. If you find you are having trouble keeping up in class, don't hesitate to let your surviving parent, the school counselor, or your teacher know. By communicating, you are allowing all of you to work together to try and help you get caught up.

SCHOOL CHALLENGES
FROM OTHERS BEFORE YOU

I did online school because of COVID so I continued that. He passed away the day that second semester started and my grades went from A's and B's to D's and F's.—Reaghan[1]

I was able to stay in the same school, with the same friends. My grades definitely slipped and looking back I don't know how much of that was me being a teenager with an attitude or the grief. Looking back, it feels like a very blurry time and I can't really separate the grief from the teenager emotions.—Travis[2]

When I started to experience grief at about 14/15, I was starting to suffer from mental health issues (mostly anxiety) quite a bit, so my grades took a small hit.—Jessica[3]

DAYDREAMING AND FANTASIZING

This is one that you really might be blindsided with. You will notice on your grief trigger days (days when something happens that suddenly triggers your grief) that sometimes you will miss your late parent so badly that you might start daydreaming or fantasizing that they really aren't gone. That maybe they got amnesia somewhere and are still walking around this Earth and that you might bump into them someday. Or that maybe the hospital staff mixed up the file and the coroner report was about someone else who just happened to have the same name as your late parent's. You might even come across someone that sounds exactly like your late mother or looks like your late father. Or you might think about what life would be like and how different it might be had your parent never passed away. Or you might even wonder if your late parent would be proud of the person you are becoming since their death.

Other scenarios include spending time rehashing what happened to your late parent and beating yourself up as if you could have made a different decision that would have saved your parent. This can be especially true if you were driving the car that got in an accident that took your late parent's life. Those around you will try to comfort you in telling you it wasn't your fault because you didn't get in the accident on purpose, but you might still struggle with blaming yourself for their death.

This is actually common, especially while you are still trying to adjust to the harsh fact that your parent is really gone. Some actually find it a therapeutic exercise and may even write letters to their late parent to tell them how their day has been going and so on. It's healthy to do but to an extent. If you find yourself spending more than half the day thinking about this, then reach out to a trusted adult or counselor. Getting too involved in this daydream or fantasy can severely set you up for disappointment. You will be flying high on cloud 9 only to crash hard if you think about this too much.

LOSS OF INTEREST IN ACTIVITIES

Before your dad died, maybe you were the soccer star of the team he coached. Now that your dad is gone and he is no longer the coach, you simply might not be interested in playing on the soccer team anymore. If your mother was the club parent of your dance team, now that she is gone, it might pain you to continue going to dance team competitions. Things you used to do and love with your parents might not be so enjoyable now that they are gone. Even if you didn't do certain activities with your parents, now that one or both of your parents are gone, it might take some time for you to be generally interested in an activity again, whether it's something you enjoyed before they died or a new activity. Again, everyone's parental death grief journey will be different. Give yourself time, no matter how long, and be patient with yourself. There will come a day when an activity will spark your interest again. Just be kind to yourself in the meantime.

STRESSED RELATIONSHIPS
WITH SURVIVING FAMILY MEMBERS

Depending on what your secondary losses might be, losing your parent can add stressed relationships with your surviving family members onto your plate. For example, when your father was alive, perhaps he was able to keep the peace between you and your younger brother. Now that your dad is gone, your mom is probably feeling overwhelmed with trying to create a new normal life for you and your brother. She might not have the time or patience to referee you and your brother, so tensions might be suddenly higher between you all. Now you and your brother are clashing more, and maybe your mom is losing a little patience trying to encourage you guys to get along. Keep in mind, that while you are grieving and navigating this new parental death territory, so are your younger brother and your mother, both in different ways. You all are grieving differently over the same person and trying to adjust to many sudden changes at once, so expect tensions to rise. Just try and be patient and understanding with one another and keep communication lines open.

My Stressed Relationships with Other Family Members

One thing that I have struggled with is how many family members and friends in my life have compared me to my late mother over the past almost three decades. My mom was a beautiful woman inside and out. She had style, wore makeup, smelled nice with the Lancôme perfume she used to wear, and she dressed nice and wore jewelry. Everyone loved her and always had something wonderful to say about her. I am not like my mother in many ways. I pretty much wear jersey shorts every day as opposed to dresses and nice clothes my mom used to wear. I don't wear makeup, barely brush my hair once a day, and if I am lucky, get a haircut once every six months, a simple $20 trim when my mother used to go to the salon and spend around $100. I only buy clothes when mine have holes in them. I have only gotten a pedicure probably about 15 times my whole life, and it was only because there was a special occasion involved like my wedding or a party. My mother used to get her nails done weekly. My mother was pretty, and I am more of a tomboy than will ever be seen by others as pretty. In my opinion, that is who I am, and my mother was who she was; however, friends and family members over the years have compared me to my mother in ways that have deeply hurt my feelings. It's like everyone wanted me to continue where my mom left off. So if she went to the salon every week to get her nails done, as her daughter, I was supposed to do the same.

I have received comments such as, "why don't you dress how your mother did? Your mother would always get her nails and hair done, how come you don't? You are nothing like your mother." I think the most hurtful comment was that last one. It hurts being compared to my mother in those ways. I know my mother is gone and everyone to this day is still sad about it, but it would have been nice if everyone accepted me for me and not compared me to who my mother was. We are two different individuals, and although we are mother and daughter and will always be through life and even through death, she is a separate person. Not all mothers and daughters like the same things and not all fathers and sons like the same things, and that's okay. I feel like because my mom died, everyone was disappointed that I was left over because I should have reminded them of memories of my mother by being exactly how she was, but I didn't fulfill their wants simply because I am who I am, which is different than my mother. That has caused a lot of self-esteem issues for me over the decades because I feel like everyone loved my mother and that I will never be good enough to fill her shoes unless I am exactly like how she was. That will never happen because I am trying to stay true to who I am.

YOUR ATTITUDE OR BEHAVIOR MIGHT CHANGE

When your mother was alive, maybe you were involved in charities, church groups, clubs, sports, and other extracurricular activities. Now that your mother is gone you have zero motivation to be involved in anything or you simply feel like you don't care about all of those causes you were previously involved in. As Peter Rabbit put it in *Peter Rabbit 2: The Runaway*, maybe before you were a goody-goody and now you are acting like a baddy-baddy. A parental death can change your attitude about life. Losing someone that close and personal to you can make everything else seem meaningless. It is your choice and responsibility for how you walk your future path and only you can decide whether you want to walk down a positive path or a negative path. If you are finding that your attitude has significantly changed after the death of your parent, reach out to a trusted adult and let them know how you are feeling. Support is important throughout this, but you can't expect people to know how to properly and responsibly help you if you don't tell them how you are honestly feeling.

DANI R. AND LOLA'S EXPERIENCE

I had already been what you could call a troubled teenager. I did drugs, drank, had horrible grades, but tried to make everyone happy. [I] didn't get caught doing 95 percent of the things I did. I tried on several occasions to commit suicide. Once with an enormous amount of [over-the-counter] sleeping pills (didn't do anything but make me sleep and tried jumping out of a moving vehicle). My boyfriend at the time grabbed my arm then pulled over. I became depressed, but didn't realize until I was a lot older that that's what was happening to me [grieving my mother's death]. I ended up living [full-time] with my aunt and uncle. I had already been living with them off and on since I was 13. I was able to stay in the same school and town. But I had no one (friends) who lost a parent so I was on my own. My sister was living with our father and there was no contact until a couple of years later.—Dani R.[4]

After my father passed away I was forced to realize how different and isolated the life of a child coping was. My school didn't really know how to help, and as I was young I also didn't know how to really act. I found myself either shutting out the topic, being overly sensitive in class, or bringing it up at somewhat inappropriate times, those inappropriate times being everyday life and conversation. It was hard in the beginning and the next two years, but eventually I learned how to "act" normal again.—Lola[5]

Figure 5.1. Sometimes losing a parent can feel isolating even if you are surrounded by others. The reality is, if you aren't surrounded by others who also lost a parent, it can indeed feel lonely at times. The key is to surround yourself by those who love and support you and are positive for you, no matter if they also lost their parent or not. Illustration by Kate Haberer

You will feel a wide range of emotions while trying to navigate through the death of your parent such as anger, abandonment, guilt, fear, worry, anxiety, depression, post-traumatic stress disorder even, and attachment to name a few. For anger, you could be angry at your parent for leaving you, the driver of the other car who killed your parent, the doctors for not saving your parent, or someone else you are angry toward regarding the death of your parent. You can be worried about your other parent dying too or worried about your future now that your parent is gone. You might struggle with abandonment because you might feel like your parent left you behind to where it can make you struggle with abandonment with others or anxiety when you step onto a plane if your parent died in a plane crash. This is one of the many normal roller-coaster rides of emotions you will feel while trying to navigate the death of your parent.

Reach out to a trusted adult, your surviving parent, a caregiver, counselor, priest, friend, or someone positive and healthy for you if you are struggling with any of these feelings so you can get the extra support that you need.

Challenges will come and go and will be different for each one of you following the death of your parent. The key is to acknowledge how you are feeling, and be open and honest to communicate with those around you to help you stay on a positive path. If you are struggling with this, think of what your late parent would want for you. Would they want you to stay on a positive path or go down a negative one?

· 6 ·

The Parental Death Dynamics

There are four parental death dynamics that you will fall under, depending on if you lost both of your parents. Are you a motherless daughter? A motherless son? A fatherless daughter? Or a fatherless son? Different dynamics pose unique challenges depending on which gender parent you lost and whether it is the same gender parent or the opposite gender parent. Extenuating circumstances can also include how close you were to your parent, if you left things unsaid with your parent, and other circumstances that can complicate the dynamic you fall under. Losing the same gender parent sparks challenges in different ways than losing your opposite gender parent can. Losing a parent is hard and life changing no matter which parent you lose, but there are different challenges that come with both.

Let's dive into the four dynamics to see which category you are. Again, everyone's parentless journey is unique to them—these are simply the four dynamics to give you an overview of some challenges that might be coming your way depending on which parent you lost.

MOTHERLESS DAUGHTER

If you are a daughter who lost her mother, you might additionally grieve what your mother never got a chance to teach you. Maybe she was there to teach you how to take care of your hair, but she wasn't there to teach you how to cook or to take care of others. So now, the harsh reality sets in that you have a disconnection and interruption in lessons you were never given the chance to be taught by your mother because your time with her was cut short. The question now is, do you have another female figure who can step in and continue these lessons that were cut short? Or do you need to teach them yourself? Or can your dad step in to teach you? Nowadays, parents are cross teaching their children whether or not they are the same gender. Sure, your dad might be the best one to teach you about throwing a spiral football or how to use tools, but when it comes to learning about tampons or bras, a female figure in your life might be a better, more experienced go to person for you. Your dad can read up on the subject of bras and tampons but not having the ability to use them might make other women who are experienced with them the better option to teach you. Same with dating boys, putting on makeup, and learning about painting your nails and doing your hair. This is not me saying dads out there can't do this. I am just simply saying that if your time was cut short with your mother before she could teach this to you, then you have options. Find the option that works best for you. Maybe asking your friend's mom if you could join in on some makeup and hair lessons, asking your grandmother to take you bra shopping, learning about your period at your school, or asking your dad about dating boys are some options. Pick the route that is best for you whether you want to learn these lessons on your own through reading books or through others in your life.

My Motherless Daughter Dynamic

Looking back, my experience was that of a pinball machine. I felt like everyone was passing me along from person to person and no one truly wanted to step up and help me. I felt alone and at times unloved, and to this day, I still struggle with the gap in lessons my mother didn't get a chance to teach me. My mother died when I was young, and so we missed the bra lesson, the period lesson, the hair and makeup lesson, the nails lesson, the cooking and child raising lesson, and the boys lesson. So here's how my lessons went after my mother died. My mother's good friend and her daughter took me bra shopping. My learning about my period lesson (after mine started during school one day) came from a mixture of my friend's mom simulating how to use tampons and pads and my stepmother trying to discuss it with me (this confused me because both women told me different things). My learning about boys happened from heartbreak and learning the hard way that there are some boys out there who are absolute jerks. My hair, makeup, and nails lesson—I will get back to you on that because to this day if I paint my nails it looks like a five-year-old painted them, I still can't figure out my hair, and I think the last time I wore makeup was for my wedding almost nine years ago that I didn't even apply myself. The cooking lesson has been a mixture from my dad, restaurants I have worked at, and teaching myself.

Looking back, I wish I had one main person who I could have counted on to step up and teach me all of these missing link lessons my mother never got a chance to teach me. Each person had a different perspective on life and that individual lesson, so getting passed around actually confused me because I didn't know whose advice to take, who was right, and in the midst of that, I sort of lost my own voice for myself. If you can swing it, try to find that one adult who will be committed to helping you with these types of lessons and girly questions you will have along the way. Someone who will be your constant and someone who won't just pick and choose what lessons or questions to help you with. It's not fun feeling like a pinball machine, trust me.

MOTHERLESS SON

If you are a son who lost his mother, you might have lost the parent who would take you to school and always be there for you when you got home. Moreover, you might wonder how you will learn how to date a girl someday when you used to watch your parents' love for each other as lessons for how you want to find the love of your life someday. Maybe your dad always gave your mom flowers, and you were really learning from their relationship for a guide on how you want to find your special person someday. Now that your mom is gone, you might be worried you won't get those exclusive lessons anymore. Or maybe your mom was always teaching you about manners and eating healthy. This is where you can express your concerns to your surviving dad, guardian, grandmother, or other trusted adult. You can also see who else you have in your life that is a positive role model who can help continue these lessons where your mother left off teaching you. Your mom might not be there to receive flowers from your dad anymore, but maybe you can watch your grandfather and grandmother exchange gifts to continue these type of relationship lessons. Maybe your aunt can step in as a mother figure (not replacing your mother) to help you continue lessons on manners. Or maybe a community member can check on you during the week after school to still give you support at home after school if your dad is still working to provide the sort of stability you had when your mother was still alive.

FATHERLESS DAUGHTER

If you are a daughter who lost your father, you might be worried about learning about dating in the future or how a man should treat you when you get older. Or perhaps your dad was giving you lessons on how to fix a car or be more independent, and now you are worried because your lessons stopped when your dad died. You can express these concerns to your mother and perhaps she can step in and help, or perhaps you have another positive male figure in your life who can continue the lessons your late father left off teaching you before he died. You might think you are going to miss out on your wedding day when your dad won't be able to walk you down the aisle. Again, maybe there is someone out there in your life who can step in. They will not be replacing your late father because no one will ever be able to do that. This male figure would be stepping in in honor of your late father to try and make this special time for you a little less difficult.

FATHERLESS SON

If you are a son who lost his father, the yearly father-son camping trip might be sad for you, especially if you think you can't go anymore because your dad is no longer here. Maybe you are worried because your dad didn't get to finish teaching you about tools, how to fix stuff around the house, or help you with your college applications. This is where your mom or guardian can step in to help as best as they can, or perhaps you have another positive male figure in your life who can step in (not replace your dad) to help show you how to use tools or fix cars like your late dad was doing before he died. Your dad might not be here to continue the lessons, but by having other positive male figures in your life, they can do your dad a favor by helping to continue your lessons. Maybe an uncle or even your friend's dad can step in and take you on the annual father-son camping trip so you don't feel left out.

IF YOU HAVE LOST BOTH PARENTS

Losing both of your parents presents multiple challenges because you lost your parent of the same gender and different one. It can be challenging, depending on how soon after one parent you lost your other one, especially if both losses happened fast when you were trying to get acclimated to your new normal.

This is where "second parents" can come in handy (positive figures in your life that can act like a parent to you). Having many second parents, or allo-parents, available to you is a blessing in disguise and can help you during your hard days. Keep in mind, however, that second parents pose some challenges, too. Not every second parent you have will be able to be available to you like your late parent was. So when you are wanting to ask them a question or spend time with them, they might be obligated with families of their own and might not be available to you as you would like them to be. Second parents have work schedules so they might not be available during the time for your mother-daughter picnic or father-son camping trip. Sometimes jealousy can strike when you are trying to spend time with your second parent, but they are spending time with their biological son or daughter instead. My best advice: Have lots of positive people in your life such as teachers, coaches, surviving family and extended family members, church figures, neighbors, and family friends, so if you try and contact one and they aren't available, try the next one, the next one, and so forth. If you put your eggs in one basket and just have one positive figure in your life, if they aren't available, it will make you feel lonelier and left out when it comes time to trying to plan events or if you are just looking for someone to talk to on your hard grief trigger days.

Figure 6.1.   Losing one parent is challenging enough but to lose both parents before you reach adulthood has unique obstacles to try and navigate. Having support and positive people you can reach out to for help and advice is really important. Illustration by Kate Haberer

TAYLOR'S UNIQUE STORY OF LOSING
BOTH PARENTS BY THE TIME SHE WAS 14

I am currently a senior in high school, and I am 17 years old. I lost my mother in December of 2012 and my father in August of 2018. I lost my mom when I was eight and I lost my dad when was 14. My mom passed away from leukemia and my father from an unexpected heart attack. My mom was diagnosed with cancer when I was five years old.

Losing her, I had time to prepare, but due to my age I could not comprehend what had happened. I was alone, my dad started drinking again, and I lashed out. If you talk to anyone who has lost a parent they will tell you their regrets, and mine is that I wish I told him how appreciative I was of him. One night, I found him passed out on the couch. I thought I had lost him, too. The next day everything changed, we talked, we cried, and he finally became my dad. After this he got help and was sober. We became extremely close and I would constantly seek him out for advice. His perseverance inspired me.

Losing my dad was one of the hardest moments of my life. When you lose one parent you see yourself as unlucky, you wonder "why me?" but you never expect to be so unlucky to lose both. There is something to be said about being an orphan even if you lose both when you are 80 years old. A week later was my father's funeral, I can only remember one thing from that day. My uncle, my dad's brother, stood up and exclaimed that he would undertake the burden of being my guardian. The air was sucked out of the room, I was terrified. He had always been jealous of my dad, and his wife thought she could replace the hole in my heart left by my mom's passing. I returned to therapy, was diagnosed with anxiety and major depressive disorder. I began to take more medications than a 70-year-old, and I would lose my appetite. I felt like I was broken.

The next three years I was on the move. I lived with friends, family, but no one could fill the hole left by my parents. Yet again I was alone. In March 2021, I moved into the house I grew up in, by myself. I think part of me expected to walk in and see my parents watching *American Idol* and smelling the cupcakes my mom would always bake on Fridays. Instead, I was greeted by scorpions, dead moths, and dust. The past three years the house had been empty; and I quickly realized that this was no longer my home. The goal was emancipation, but the means to get there were close to impossible.

My parents loved music, and after they passed, I found it comforting to listen to their music. I had always despised my dad's punk rock classics, but I found myself listening to them constantly. There have been ups and downs, but I would say I am doing pretty good right now. Although there have been times where I substance abused, thought about and attempted suicide, and had to go into a mental health facility.

I have gone to counseling regularly twice a week since my father died; I was also put on medications. Through therapy I was diagnosed with major depressive disorder, PTSD, and anxiety. Talk therapy is something I will do for the rest of my life and encourage everyone to participate in. My situation is unique, and I have a hard time relating to other 17-year-olds; however, I know a handful of other kids who have lost a parent and am able to talk to them about it. I am really bad at comparing my situation to others and making my problems seem small, so group therapy was not super healthy for me. However, it is a good way to realize you are not alone. I feel like I missed out on getting to know the beautiful person that was my mom. I miss my dad's advice and being able to talk about anything with him. I always wonder who will walk me down the aisle or who will help me with my makeup at my senior prom. I feel [gypped] by these special moments everyone else gets with their parents. I struggle with letting my family in because in the past they have made me feel like I need to replace my mom and dad. Now, I take a lot of comfort in older girl cousins, my dad's close friends, and my boyfriend's parents who have become my pseudo family.[1]

Remember that each dynamic offers unique challenges and each teen or young adult is going to grieve and cope differently. No two stories or scenarios are alike.

II

COPING WITH
PARENTAL DEATH

 $\mathcal{N}$ ow that you are starting to gain a better understanding and background of losing a parent at a young age, it's important to know that you are not facing this tragic situation alone and that there are lots of different types of support available to you out there. Depending on your new home situation, you might be worried about seeking support due to your new financial situation or, other factors, such as your other surviving family members who might be grieving in a complicated way or your homework load from school, and more. How you cope as you forge ahead is extremely important, and it is imperative to do it in a healthy way for the sake of your future. It might seem obvious to cope in a healthy way, but you'd be surprised how it will be easy to think on a hard day that making a bad decision might make you feel better. Getting enough sleep, eating healthy, drinking plenty of water, self-care, and quiet time are really important, but you might struggle with all of these on some days. This is why it is important to know all of the available options and methods of support and coping mechanisms you have, so on those hard days you can have them readily accessible for you to use to keep you on a healthy path. It's not like school teaches a class on how to live life after your parent dies when you are still young and dependent on them, so when a parental death happens, everyone is sort of in uncharted waters. Read on, as I am going to throw you many life rafts to help you find your way and stay on a good path.

· 7 ·

Positive Coping Methods

$\mathcal{L}$earning how to cope with parental death in a positive way is essential to your overall well-being. Grief of the death of your parent is going to be a lifelong journey, and you will experience hard days, challenging days, and days that can trigger your grief for the death of your parent almost out of nowhere. Don't get me wrong, there will also be plenty of good days where you will find happiness remembering your late parent, but having positive coping methods on hand can ensure you stay on a lifelong healthy and positive coping path. Let's dive a little more into this.

Let's say that you are watching a movie on TV, and a commercial breaks for perfume. It just happens to be the same perfume your late mother wore. I know it sounds strange, but seeing that perfume on screen suddenly can bring back memories of when you watched your mother put it on and even a sense of smell by remembrance can occur. This is an example of a grief trigger. It can send you into instant teary-eyed sadness or give you a smile because it brings up pleasant memories of your late mother. There are many ways that you can handle this trigger moment. Because this is the positive coping methods chapter, let's stay on point. A positive way to cope with this is perhaps to look at the photo album and reminisce of the memories you had with your late mother, perhaps call your grandmother to chat, or go out and take a walk and look up and smile almost as if you are telling your mother, "hi." You could also go for a jog or decide to volunteer your time at church or your school.

Let's say another type of scenario occurs. On your way home from school your dad had to take a different route home and he had to pass by the hospital where your mother died. If the loss is still new, this can send you on a grief frenzy where you have uncontrollable sadness arise and potentially even anger toward the doctors and nurses who couldn't save your mother. You get home and you run to your room and shut the door. This is where your positive coping methods playbook comes in handy. You are super upset, but you know that coloring calms you down, so you reach for your favorite coloring book and start coloring away. Or perhaps you reach for a CD that you and your mom used to listen to together, or you put on your mom's favorite movie and snuggle under a blanket to feel comforted.

Having positive coping methods ready and accessible can keep you on a healthy positive coping path throughout your life. Gather and acknowledge what are healthy and positive ways to cope with the death of your parent, so when a challenging day or grief trigger arises, whether you are home or out and about, you can reach for those methods to help you get through your grief moment. Remember that a moment is only temporary and the moment will pass, even though it seems difficult and unbearable. Again, find healthy positive coping methods that work best for you. Some examples include listening to music, exercising, watching a movie, reading a book, shopping (under a budget of course), cooking a healthy meal, volunteering your time, spending time with friends or family, writing in your diary, praying, doing chores, and more. Check out chapter 10 for supplemental therapy methods that can give you more ideas.

POSITIVE COPING METHODS

If you find yourself having a difficult grief trigger or grief moment, reach for one of the following positive coping methods to help you pass the moment:

- Look at pictures and photo albums of your late parent
- Call a family member to chat
- Take a walk, look up, and say "hi" to your late parent
- Take a jog
- Volunteer at your church or school

- Color a coloring book
- Listen to comforting music
- Snuggle under a blanket and watch a comforting movie
- Read a book
- Go shopping
- Cook a healthy meal
- Write in a diary or journal
- Pray
- Do chores

A NOTE ABOUT COPING THROUGH SOCIAL MEDIA

Nowadays, it seems like everyone has at least one social media account. It's not like how back in the day everyone called each other or sent letters via the mail. Times have changed, and I get that. Social media can be good, but in some ways bad to cope with parental death. Because the focus in this chapter is on positive coping methods, I will only discuss the positive about it in this chapter. See chapter 8 for the negative side of coping through social media. The good part about coping through social media is that chances are you can connect with many friends and relatives who knew your late parent. Maybe you can start a Facebook page in honor of your late parent where all those that knew your dad or mom can post pictures or memories of your parent. This can be a page that is private to all those who knew your parent and a place where you all can keep their memory alive, but where you also might see pictures someone else shared that you never saw of your parent before or to learn about memories others had with your late parent. You can also use social media to seek social media parental death support groups that might be out there or to seek out organizations that might pertain to coping with grief. You might even come across a volunteer organization that focuses on the cause of death that happened to your parent to where you might want to get involved in to help give back to others in honor of your late parent. There can be many positive scenarios that can come out of using social media to help you cope.

· 8 ·

Negative Coping Methods

$\mathcal{S}$o, let's say it's a Friday night, and you are angry because all of your buddies are hanging out with their dads at the annual father-son BBQ that you and your dad used to attend. This is the first year without your dad and the first year you won't be able to attend the BBQ with your dad, and no other male figure in your life stepped in so you could still attend. You are angry, hurt, and feel alone. You have the urge to grab your mother's cigarette pack and light one up, or you feel like destroying a car with a bat because you just feel so mad. What if that one cigarette you decide to light up leads you down a path of addiction? Or that bat to the car gets you in trouble with police and suddenly you have a criminal record before you have even graduated high school? What will that do to your future? How do you think that would make your late parent feel if they were still alive today?

What if your boyfriend just cheated on you and left you for your best friend, and you needed someone to talk to about it. In particular, you want to talk to your mother who would always give you relationship advice when she was still alive. You are hurt, you are heartbroken, but suddenly another guy steps in to give you some attention you are desperately needing. What if you take that moment too far, only to find out he was just using you for a one-night stand, and suddenly you are pregnant and alone before you even graduate high school?

Moments are temporary, and moments can hurt so bad and can trigger the pain you feel from missing your late parent. These moments can make your emotions go all over the place, but if you don't take care of your emotions in a healthy way, it can lead you down a negative path. It is important to stay away from negative coping methods, such as using drugs, drinking alcohol, participating in risky sexual behavior, or crime, so you don't make that temporary moment of pain and grief a permanent negative mark on your future.

DANI R.'S EXPERIENCE

Looking back, I was a teenager [during a time where there was] no understanding of depression. My coping mechanism was drinking and doing drugs, yet still trying to be a good girl and not get in trouble. Honestly, I don't think I realized I was depressed [until I was older]. I was told that I was emotional, and that was my problem. At the time, me drinking and [doing] drugs was my only way to cope. Had I been able to maybe see a therapist that would have helped, I'm sure. But I also look at even through the bad that I did, it's what made me who I am today.[1]

It is important to recognize these feelings you might have and to have backups in place, so you choose and reach for positive healthy coping methods and not negative ones. Let the trusted adults who love and care for you know that you might be struggling with anger, feeling alone, or feeling lost so they can help you stay on a healthy, positive coping path. Have someone who you can call in that moment you are about to do something you might regret so they can talk you out of making a decision that can negatively alter your life. Stay away from peers who might pressure you into drinking, doing drugs, or smoking cigarettes and make sure you have good friends and a good support system in place to guide you. If you feel so much anger to where you want to break a car window with a bat, instead why not channel that anger by joining a gym and taking a boxing class? Or if you want to destroy a building by using graffiti, why not sign up for an art class instead? You are the only person responsible for the decisions you make and the only one who gets to decide what path you will stay on in life while navigating grieving the death of your parent. Will you choose a positive, healthy path or a negative, unhealthy one? The choice is yours and yours alone. With choice comes great responsibility because each decision you make can impact your future.

A NOTE ABOUT COPING THROUGH SOCIAL MEDIA

Like I mentioned in chapter 7, social media can be good but in some ways bad to cope with parental death. Because this chapter focuses on negative coping methods, I will only discuss the negative about it. See the previous chapter for the positive side of coping through social media.

Let's say you post something heartfelt about your late parent, but you didn't make it a private post to those who knew your parent, and someone else on your Facebook wall or Instagram page comments in a way that is not respectful to your late parent or does not support positive comments. This can really hurt your feelings. What if you post a memory about your parent and that one family member who is always causing drama chimes in and tries to tell you that your memory of what happened is wrong? Social media arguing will not help you cope in a good way and can actually really upset you. The death of your parent is going to feel sensitive for you, so if you don't have sensitive people on your social media friends' lists, I would advise that you be careful what you post or at least make your post about your parents private to those who loved and knew your late parent, so everyone can be respectful, instead of opening comments to a peer from three years ago who is still on your friends list but that you might not talk to anymore. Also, be careful on social media by thoroughly checking who you are connecting with. A Facebook group could say they are affiliated with a certain grief or health organization, but in reality, be a scam or not be the official organization you think to which you are connecting. Also, be careful with grief forums, especially those geared toward children, teens, or young adults. Remember that just because someone says they are 17 like you are, does not mean they are truly 17. They could be 45, 60, or even an 8-year-old. If you decide to use social media to help you cope, I strongly suggest you do it cautiously. In the end, it might be safer for you to at least visit an organization's website directly so you know it's officially and legitimately the organization you are trying to reach, and it might be more sensitive for you to create private spaces on social media for friends or family members only to share pictures and memories of your late parent rather than publicly. Keep in mind too that when you post something online, it is really hard to remove it.

· 9 ·

Forms of Therapy Options

$\mathscr{P}$erhaps you have heard of counselors but have never officially seen one. Maybe you heard about it from a movie or one of your friends described their experience. This can give you both good and bad feelings regarding a counselor. Each person who sees a counselor will have their own unique experience because each counselor is different, just like the same goes for each person who sees a counselor will have different needs. Think about your teachers at school. Not all teachers teach using the same methods, just like not every student learns in the same way. The same goes for counseling. Let's dive a little more into counseling.

There are three main types of counselors someone your age will most likely be familiar with. There's your school counselor, there's an outside of school counselor such as a psychologist, and then there's a psychiatrist. The main difference between a psychologist and a psychiatrist is that a psychiatrist can prescribe medication, but a psychologist cannot. Most counselors see you in person, but there are additional options, especially nowadays, where you can see a tele-counselor over the internet. Let's learn more about the three main types of counselors, shall we?

SCHOOL COUNSELOR

A school counselor works in your school and is there to help you with anything you're struggling with. They typically do not charge your guardian money for you to see them because they are a part of your school's staff just like your teacher, principal, librarian, and others. The counselor works with your teachers and your schedule to give you some one-on-one time with them to talk about things you might be struggling with. In this case, they'll help you navigate the death of your parent and any secondary losses or challenges you might be facing. Depending on your needs and level of comfort, they might want to meet with you weekly, bi-weekly, or monthly. In some cases, they might communicate with your teachers and surviving parent or guardian but only with regard to your best interest. They are considered a safe adult to talk to where you can share your feelings. They will protect your privacy; you just have to be open to communication with them and be honest with your feelings. Let's face it, sometimes you might not want to tell your parent or teacher something. This is where the school counselor comes in, to where you might feel more comfortable talking to them instead.

LOLA AND THAD'S COUNSELING EXPERIENCE

I haven't seen [a counselor] regularly. I did talk with the school counselor at my school when I had just lost my father, but it instead made things worse. I felt like they didn't understand me and were somewhat helpless in how to help me, and because of that at a young age I developed a distrust for counselors. After that I've tried to keep away and find ways I knew I would cope well, which was peer to peer support and outside activities.—Lola[1]

We didn't get any professional counseling and I wish we had. In some ways we were damaged, and grades did slip. Looking back on it, Mom was the one in our family who dreamed for us. If she had lived, we would have been much more whole and healthy. We would have been more successful in school and in life in general if she had lived, so her death created a void that no one else could fill.—Thad[2]

PSYCHOLOGIST

Outside of your school, you and your guardian or surviving parent might want to help you navigate your grief by having you see a psychologist or outside of school counselor. This is a counselor that does require payment and you see in similar ways as your school counselor—either weekly, bi-weekly, monthly, or whatever you all agree is in the best interest for you and your needs. A psychologist is someone who is educationally trained to help you work through life struggles and challenges and who can provide helpful resources and tools to support you. They are also considered a safe adult to talk to. Again, it's important to be open and honest with your feelings. They are there to help you and not harm you. If you are ever uncomfortable talking to them about something, all you have to do is tell them that and they can move on to something else to help you.

EXPERIENCES FROM SEEING A PSYCHOLOGIST

I do remember a couple of the sessions my dad and nan had with a child psychologist after she passed. But I mostly remember being given child friendly books on loss and coping. I've seen a [counselor] for mental health issues and would mention my mum, but it would kind of be pushed aside. I've more recently looked at getting one to one support with dealing with this late grief. I haven't heard many stories similar to mine when someone has lost a parent at a really young age and then be affected a lot through teenage/young adult years so trying to relate to things or get help has been difficult.—Jessica[3]

[It] Took me 10 years, but yes I am now [seeing a counselor]. Counseling has changed my world. Literally. I wish I had done it sooner.—Sharon[4]

I did see a counselor for a while, but it felt impersonal, and I always felt more comfortable talking with my sister. I feel like I have support from close family members, but not from friends. I can't blame them though as I understand it can be hard to bring up.—Chase[5]

I did seek counseling but only as an adult and then I still had my high school friend who helped me a lot. In fact, she had actually become a psychologist and still helps me to this day. I didn't like counseling at first. I felt like they were prying into my business, and I didn't trust them. I didn't know how to share my feelings. No one had ever asked me or taught me how. The first few times I couldn't speak to the counselor, so I wrote things down and then when she talked to me about my feelings etc. the sessions started to get easier and the more I went the easier it got and the more I talked and we talked about things the better I felt.—Georgianne[6]

[I] have [seen a counselor], but I feel like I started too late. I felt I "was fine" but didn't realize some of the deep-seated feelings and thoughts that were not just feeling sad that ended up shaping who I am in positive and negative ways.—Travis[7]

I once saw a counselor after I had my daughter. I was going through some very bad Premenstrual Dysphoric Disorder (PMDD) and a bad relationship with my daughter's father. I went about five times and even once brought my daughter to the meeting. I do not feel the meetings helped. They were focused on my anger issues and not on my depression and loss of my mother.—Dani R.[8]

PSYCHIATRIST

Outside of your school, you and your guardian or surviving parent might want to help you navigate your grief by having you see a psychiatrist. A psychiatrist is an educationally trained professional who you can talk to like a psychologist or school counselor, but they are the only one who can legally and ethically prescribe medication if they and your guardian or surviving parent think it is in your best interest. They require payment, and again you can see them weekly, biweekly, or monthly. They are also considered a safe adult to talk to.

If you have never seen a counselor before, it's understandable if you are a little nervous or scared to do so for your first time, especially if one of your friends shared their not so happy experience with you. Again, every person seeing a counselor is different and has different needs and every counselor is different. You're only going to know what it's like when you experience it yourself. The key to counseling is to be open and honest with how you're feeling and to communicate if something is making you uncomfortable.

My Counseling Experience

My mother was sick for the last few years of her life. Our family started counseling while she was sick and dying. Our counselor ended up becoming a good family friend of ours. Her name was Jane. We would see Jane once a month individually. After my mom died, we continued to see Jane once a month. I was comfortable talking to her because she knew my whole family and we had been seeing her for a few years already. It made me feel comfortable knowing that she knew my mother before she died, too. Jane was a counselor outside of school. Inside of school, I started seeing the principal and the school counselor monthly after my mom died. I was comfortable with them too because they had been at my school for the past eight years while I was attending. They also all knew my mother when she was alive. When we left California and moved to Arizona, I lost my two school counselors and Jane so that's when my counseling progress ended.

Counseling will definitely be a unique experience, but you won't know what it is like until you officially try it yourself. If you are interested in trying counseling, reach out to a trusted adult, your surviving parent, your caregiver, or your teacher so they can help get you started.

· 10 ·

Supplemental Therapy Options

So, let's say it's 2:30 a.m. You just woke up from having flashbacks from when your parent was sick and the members in your house are sleeping, your friends and other relatives are sleeping, and even if you are seeing a counselor, chances are you might not be able to call your counselor at 2:30 a.m. You could try going back to sleep, but that might be hard because of how upset you are. How do you handle that moment of grief when everyone you want to reach out to is not available?

You find the strength within you to learn how to be there for yourself.

This won't always come easily, especially at first, but through time, you will get better at being there for yourself. You will learn about depending on yourself more than depending on others, because the reality is, other people in your life can not always be available to you 24/7. And this is why I am going to teach you about supplemental therapy options.

What is supplemental therapy? You might have already heard of it, without even realizing it. Think of retail therapy. When you are having a frustrating day, we have all gone shopping or gone out to dinner to give ourselves a pick me up at one point or another. This is what supplemental therapy is. There are several supplemental therapy options that you can choose from that are practical to where you do not have to depend on anyone to access and use. Retail therapy is a popular one, but that does not mean that everyone likes to go shopping to feel better. And that does not mean to go max out your credit card or allowance trying to cope when you're having difficult grief moments either. As with anything, it is healthy to have a balance and set limits. Let me walk you through some supplemental therapy options so this way, when you have a rough time at 2:30 a.m., or throughout anytime during the day, you have a plethora of options to choose from to help yourself cope independently.

MOVIE THERAPY

There are several movies out there in many types of genres that can help you cope independently when you might be having a rough grief moment. Some of you might want to watch a comedy or a chick flick to cheer up. Others might want an action movie or a documentary. Only you know what type of movie can help cheer you up. However, might I suggest not just going for traditional genres while you're browsing your Blu-ray collection, Netflix selections, or Amazon prime videos. Is there a movie that would comfort you that perhaps you and your late parent used to watch together? Or a movie that reminds you of you and your late parent or perhaps something fun you both used to do together? You can even go a step further and pick a movie that has a fictional character who lost a parent like you did so you can relate to them on the big screen. Lola shares, "The movie I remember being very stark to me for coping was *Big Hero 6*. It was a wonderfully done movie that centered around loss, and coping. Seeing Hero struggle made me feel human, and not as alone."[1] Check out appendix B for some more suggestions.

And you don't just have to stop at movies, as there are plenty of TV shows that can serve a comforting purpose as well. Here are some suggestions that include characters who lost a parent:

- *Full House*
- *Fuller House*
- *The Flash*
- *Green Arrow*
- *Smallville*
- *WandaVision*

Figure 10.1.   Sometimes watching movies can be comforting because they might remind us of when we used to watch the same movie with our late parent. In some cases, certain actors or actresses remind us of our parents in some way. And other times, we can relate to a fictional character who also lost their parent in the movie. Illustration by Kate Haberer

THAD AND SHARON'S EXPERIENCE

If you'd like a visual, [my mother] looked a lot like Queen Elizabeth, so when I see Queen Elizabeth on the television, I think that is what Mom would look like if she were still alive.—Thad[2]

Buffy the Vampire Slayer, Firefly, Big Bang Theory, and *Survivor* were other shows Dad and I loved watching together . . . and those kept us together. In fact, when [*Big Bang Theory*] ended in 2019, it was in some ways like my dad died all over again. It felt like my heart got ripped out, losing one of the last links to him.—Sharon[3]

My Movie of Choice

One movie that I love to watch when I'm having a difficult grief moment is *You've Got Mail* starring Meg Ryan and Tom Hanks. It's considered to be a chick flick, but I enjoy it because I can relate to the character of Kathleen Kelly (played by Ryan). She inherited her late mother's bookstore and has tried to keep her mother's memory alive by keeping the bookstore open and reliving memories with patrons who frequent the store who also knew Kathleen's mother. I love books and it reminds me of when my mom was alive when I watch it. It comforts me and reminds me of going to the bookstore and even Scholastic book fairs with my mom.

BIBLIOTHERAPY

Like movie therapy, bibliotherapy dives into reading books to help comfort you while you are having a challenging or difficult grief moment. Again, you can choose books of any genre, but you can also choose books that have fictional characters that lost a parent like you did so you can relate to them (see appendix A for suggestions). You can also pick up a book that you and your parent used to read together when you were younger, or you might find comfort in reading a book you know your late parent enjoyed reading. Or maybe there was a book your late parent mentioned they always wanted to read but never had a chance to read it. Or you simply just want to get lost in the words another author wrote. Through reading, you can feel connected to your late parent during your grief moment.

COMFORT BOOKS OF OTHERS

I ended up getting deep into Anne Rice *Vampire Chronicles* and anything Stephen King. Reading was my way of escape.—Dani R.[4]

I think I always found solace in the *Percy Jackson* and *Harry Potter* series. I remember when I was 10, I was very much obsessed with the series a *School for Good and Evil*. I guess the thing that really stuck out with all of them was that they were very much fantasy. And escape from reality I needed.—Lola[5]

I had a book as a child called *The Velveteen Rabbit* that my nan said helped me understand loss at a younger age.—Jessica[6]

My Book Preferences

I have never had the chance to visit Italy and I am not sure if I will ever be given the opportunity to do so in my life; however, when my mother was young, she went on a trip to Italy. I have seen the pictures and Italy looks so beautiful, and my mother looked so happy and that she really had a good time vacationing there. Because I love reading, I find myself often picking up books that have a location in Italy. I think it makes me feel connected to my mom when I read them. I feel like when I read about books based in Italy, that in some ways I can daydream that I was on that trip to Italy with my mom when she was younger. It is a real treat when I am reading Italian novels and I come across something my mother did on her trip; it always comforts me, and I smile and sometimes even shed a tear.

ART THERAPY

You are never too old to color. Coloring books are so relaxing, enjoyable, and therapeutic. Grab a coloring book with crayons, color pencils, or markers and just let your creative side pour out during your grief moment. It does not just stop at coloring. Paint, sculpt, sew, make crafts, even Play-Doh or modeling clay can do wonders for you. Maybe your late mother was sewing something that was left unfinished when she died. Why not pick up where she left off and finish it? It is hard to explain, but there is a wonderful connection in partaking in hobbies your late parent enjoyed or finishing something they started, but perhaps were not able to finish.

WRITING THERAPY

Writing out your feelings in a journal or diary can be therapeutic as well. You could even go the creative route and write short stories or even poetry. Some find it comforting to actually write a letter to their late parent that is like they are having a conversation with them in the present, telling them how their day went, sharing what they miss about them, or in some cases apologizing if their last moment did not go as they wish it had. Writing during your challenging or difficult grief moment can be a form of creative expression that can help you help yourself.

My Writing Therapy Preference

I enjoy writing creative fiction pieces that feature characters who lost a parent young like I did. I pull memories I had with my mother and incorporate pieces of my mom in my stories. It is therapeutic, and I have several fiction pieces I have written for small children, teens, and young adults that I am actively seeking to publish to share with others to comfort other parentless children, teens, and young adults.

MUSIC THERAPY

We all have good days and bad days, and when grief is involved, there are especially hard days at times. Listening to a song that your late parent used to sing or even just a song that you can resonate with the words can be really comforting. Perhaps playing an instrument relaxes you or watching musical concerts helps. Whether singing along or just listening, music can help comfort you during your grief moment. Song choices do not have to necessarily be about songs of the loss of your parent. The music part of this can be songs that remind you of you and your late parent spending time together or even a song you knew was their favorite or a song you both used to listen to together. Or, if you yourself are a musician, why not write a song in tribute to your late parent yourself? It could be a therapeutic exercise.

MUSIC EXPERIENCES FROM OTHERS

I grew up in a household where music was prevalent. The stereo was always on, and my parents shared their favorite artists with me all the time. When my mom died, I started to seek and connect with words and lyrics from others who had taken the time to put their experiences of losing a loved one to song. I connected to and committed them to memory or tried hard to translate what they were saying. Today it is still a huge part of my life, but I also know that other types of creative and physical outlets help me work through any idea, especially grief and being able to separate it from life.

I have a playlist now that I refer to as "Death Jams" (https://mydeathjams.com/). I was heavily into music and started cultivating a list of songs by people that were about the death of a loved one. I still use this list and it has grown and is very, very important to me.—Travis[7]

I listened to a lot of Linkin Park; a LOT of Linkin Park. *Leave Out All the Rest* was the one song I could listen to and immediately cry.—Sharon[8]

I recommend a Johnny Cash song called *The Highwayman*. As a matter of fact, I recommend all Johnny Cash songs. His American series from 10 or 15 years ago especially.—Thad[9]

As I grew older, I found coping in classical music. Chopin and Debussy were always something I listened to when I was feeling upset.—Lola[10]

Song wise I know a few that she liked that I would listen to, to feel closer to her. I've always loved music and had a strong connection with music, so this helps the most at times. And crying is perfectly normal.—Jessica[11]

The song, *I Can Only Imagine* by Mercy Me was written by a man who lost his dad. I identified strongly with that song and took comfort in the beautiful imagery of the word portrait of heaven.—Liz[12]

My mom said that my dad used to sing *Baby Face* by Sammy Kaye to me.—Debbie[13]

Listening to music as a form of supplementary therapeutic technique does not have to have lyrics as it could just be listening to jazz or classical music. If there are lyrics, the songs do not have to have a parental death aspect in them. Maybe the song was a song you and your late mother used to jam out to while baking cookies or a song your dad always sung during Christmas time. Remember that this is your grieving journey and no one else's. You get to decide what music soothes your soul.

RETAIL THERAPY

Probably the most popular one, retail therapy, is the one that can provide temporary comfort with the click of a button or a swipe of a card. Buying something that makes you happy or even shopping somewhere you and your late parent used to go can comfort you. Just make sure

Figure 10.2. Music is another form of therapy that can help comfort you while you are navigating your grief. Whether listening to a song that was your parent's favorite, singing one that mentions grief and loss throughout it, or just listening to a genre of music can be really calming. Illustration by Kate Haberer

you set limits, so you don't spend as much money because your mind is telling you to spend while you're seeking comfort. I think we'd all easily spend thousands of dollars to make ourselves feel better, even if it was just for a moment. I think we all wish we had money like that to spend; however, that is not reality.

My Retail Therapy Experience

I was a young girl, and my mom and I would often go shopping at the mall together. Everyone at all the stores we would frequent knew my mother well and knew us by name. So, my mom started a tradition with me. Each time we went to the mall, we would stop by the Mrs. Fields cookie store and get cinnamon sugar cookies. It was such a happy tradition that I loved sharing with my mom. After she died, every time I would go visit the mall, I continued getting a cinnamon sugar cookie because it made me feel like I was keeping our mother-daughter tradition alive. I grew sad however, when the Mrs. Fields store at the mall closed, but now I do a similar tradition with my little one each time we visit the bookstore.

COOKING THERAPY

Cooking for yourself is not only healthier but more rewarding than if you constantly eat out or have other people cook for you all the time. There is something relaxing about allowing yourself to be creative to make a new recipe and add your own style to the presentation of it or changing up the ingredients a bit. Maybe on top of that, you and your late parent used to cook together or you used to watch them cook. Being in the kitchen and wearing the same apron they wore, listening to the same background music they listened to when they used to cook can make you feel connected to them. If you always baked cookies together for the holidays, keep the tradition alive.

VOLUNTEERING THERAPY

For some, good old-fashioned volunteering might do the trick. Putting all of your energy and grief during your hard times toward a greater cause helps heal your heart in ways you did not think or know were possible. Serving others who might have it as bad as you feel you do or worse does something unique for your mind, body, and soul.

LOLA'S VOLUNTEERING PROJECT

[The] Minus One [Project] is an idea I've had since I lost my father. After not having the best professional help, I wanted to make a safe space for kids who have suffered a loss, to interact, ask questions and relax. It has gone through many stages, from an idea to a website to a blog! I've worked with several organizations specializing in grief, learning more about the field of child grief and how I can help with my idea. At the moment, I'm working with VIP (the violence intervention program) to see how I can expand and help locally. I have also been thinking about creating a discord server for children as a beta for my idea. It's been many years of work but through it I've learned a lot about the world of entrepreneurship. I am also thinking about creating an illustrated book on child grief. In short, Minus One is an organization that focuses on peer-to-peer coping. At my school I run a peer-to-peer club called Plus One, that offers a confidential safe space for students suffering from loss or any trauma.—Lola[14]

PRAYER THERAPY

No matter what your religion is, prayers can be a powerful form of therapy. Talking to God, reading biblical scripture, blogs from preachers, or just sitting in peace and quiet and asking your higher power what it is you need to help heal your soul. Prayer can be powerful when you are struggling during a grief moment. Liz shares, "Psalm 46 became my go to verse when my heart hurt. 'God is our refuge and strength, a very present help in times of trouble. Therefore, we shall not fear.'"[15]

How I Found a Closeness to God through My Pain

At first when my mother died, I found myself really mad at God. I used to go to church with my mom all the time and I prayed all the time, so when my mother died, I felt like God was being unfair to me to have taken her from me when I loved her so much. Shortly after, even during my first year after my mother died, I realized that my way of thinking was wrong and even selfish. I started realizing that God did not take my mom away from me. Instead, I realized He saved her from her pain. She was in a lot of pain and her quality of life was no longer good or positive. I have made peace with God since I was almost 10 years old that I was not mad at Him for taking her away from me, but instead I have expressed gratitude toward Him ever since for releasing my mother from her pain and unhappiness.

PET THERAPY

Pets can heal our hearts in unexplainable ways. They always seem to know when we need a hug and having a pet can be therapeutic. If you are having a difficult grief moment, give your dog extra pets, give your cat extra treats, or feed the ducks at the nearby pond. You could always volunteer at the animal shelter to give a little extra love to animals and pets who do not have a home.

LAUGHTER THERAPY

It might sound unusual but a lot of kids, teenagers, and young adults cope with the death of their parent in a humorous way. I know it seems disrespectful, but hear me out. Maybe your late parent was a jokester, so hearing jokes or watching their old comedy performances might make you smile. Watching other comedians crack jokes or watching a funny movie might help lift your spirits, too.

These are just some of the many different forms of supplemental therapy methods there are out there. Everyone is different and everyone's needs when it comes to processing grief are different than others. Find accessible and practical therapeutic supplementary methods that work for you that can be easily available on the days when you need to be there for yourself and reach for these positive methods.

· 11 ·

Support

$\mathcal{H}$aving support can make you feel less alone in your parental death grief journey. It is beneficial to have multiple outlets of support available to you in case you need it. Think of it in terms of an acrobat. They fly high into the air with little to no support; however, if they fall, they have a safety net below to catch them. Support from those around you is your safety net. You might think you are grieving well when suddenly a grief trigger hits you and you break down crying. You didn't think you needed support anymore, but at least you have people in your "safety net" that you can still turn to.

SUPPORT GROUPS

Support groups can be a safety net for you. Check out your school and local community to see what type of support groups might be offered to help you. Maybe there is a motherless daughter group on meetup.com or a local fatherless son group on Facebook. As with anything, consult a trusted adult to make sure the support group you are seeking is safe for you to join. Check out local hospital bereavement groups, nonprofit support groups or bereavement camps, or online support group forums. See the resources section at the end of this book for some helpful suggestions.

SCHOOL SUPPORT

School support can come in many different forms. It can be from your teachers, your coaches, the administrative staff, and the school counselor; it can even come from the janitor who also lost his father at a young age who you can relate to; or it can come from another one of your peers who also lost their mother at a young age like you did. Having support at school, where you typically spend most of your time during the week, can be a huge help. You could have a grief trigger smack in the middle of class, so it is helpful that your teachers are supportive if you need to excuse yourself to go out in the hall for 15 minutes for some extra quiet time.

LOLA'S EXPERIENCE WITH SUPPORT

The role [of support] has passed to different people as time goes on. People-wise I remember in eighth grade I had three teachers who treated me like I was their daughter and who I saw as father figures. A Humanities teacher, my cooking teacher, and my art/ PE teacher. It was a little ironic because we had a school counselor but I never sought her out when I needed help. They filled that missing part and I was grateful for them. Being able to have that support was really important for me.[1]

FAMILY SUPPORT

Family support is one of the most important forms of support I hope you have. Whether you have a supportive guardian or surviving parent, sibling, grandparent, aunt or uncle, cousin, second cousin, family support is important because they have a connection to your late parent. Maybe you have family support from your uncle, who is also the brother of your late mother. Having this supportive connection can really be beneficial to you because they knew your parent and might remember things they would say or advice they would give that can be passed down to you. Or they can share stories or memories of your late parent that can help comfort you on your tough grieving days.

MORE STORIES OF SUPPORT

The only support I've really had so far has been my nan (on my dad's side). She is the only family member that really knows how much I've struggled over the past few years and is slightly upset with my dad for expecting me to just always move on like he did. When my dad and nan saw the child psychologist they were told that her death could affect me again in my teenage years/ young adulthood and that is normal and somewhat expected in scenarios such as mine. I'd say that my nan (on my dad's side) stepped up the most, since my dad was in the army, he worked a lot so my nan gave up working at times to look after me. My nan and I have always been very close because of this and if I ever need help, I always call her or speak to her first but I wouldn't really say it's a motherly bond I have with her, I'd say it's more of just a really close grandmother bond. I think as well that because my nan lost her dad at 13, we've always been close in the sense of losing a parent young.—Jessica[2]

My mom has been my biggest support. She's wonderful. She has been such an incredible balance of support and nurture and strength. She never let me use my sorrow as an excuse not to work hard or do what needed to be done. But she is always there to share the joy and sadness of memories when they come up.—Liz[3]

My family, of course, was grieving with me, so we all supported each other. I had my brother and my tight knit family to talk to whenever I needed it.—Lola[4]

OUTSIDE SUPPORT

Outside support is also helpful because it includes the umbrella of help that falls into the "other" category aside from support groups, school, and family support, but that is extremely important for you. It can include your church, your neighborhood or community, your club sports team, and more.

STORIES OF OUTSIDE SUPPORT

My mom had some friends at church who really took me under their wing. The women from her Bible study did lots of things to make me feel loved and cared for. They took me out to dinner, they attended my high school graduation, they made special time to just talk with me and check in with me. It meant more to me than I can express.—Liz[5]

My friends, my closest ones, have been there for me since day one, some quite literally finding me right after I had lost my father. Currently I've found support in my father's closest friend, who lives in New York. He checks up on us when he can, and always makes me laugh with stories of my father. I remember when he met the boy I was seeing last spring and he immediately put on the parental figure attire. It was so sweet to see, knowing my father would never get the chance to do so and I was grateful for him.—Lola[6]

My church family were very important. About 30 years after Mom died I met an older woman and introduced myself. She [said she knew my mother]. She asked how I was and how was my brother and sister. I told her we were fine. She had taught school with my mother and had just assumed that without her we would have all ended up in prison or something. She was pleasantly surprised that we had turned out okay. I give all the credit to my father, my aunts, cousins, etc. As well as our minister and his care for us. Church was very important in keeping us on some kind of positive path.—Thad[7]

My Story—Finding Support through a Yearbook

One day, when I was having a difficult grief moment and felt like no one was there for me, I decided to look through my mom's yearbooks. I started reading all of the people who signed her yearbook, trying to learn more about her and the person she was when she was younger. While looking through the comments, I got an idea to start plugging in some of their names on Facebook to try and see if I could locate any of them. Out of many attempts, I was able to connect with two who thankfully did not think I was a creeper trying to reach out to them in the way that I did. One, Debbie, has become a wonderful second mother to me. She and my mother were good friends, and she was even part of my mom's wedding party for my parents' marriage. Over the last few years since we connected, she has been absolutely wonderful sharing old stories, pictures, and memorabilia about and from my mom's time with me. I appreciate connecting with Debbie so much and feel like it's a gift from God and my mother to give me someone who cares for me like a mother but who is also connected to my mother's past. It's such a beautiful gift that's hard to explain. It's like I am revisiting my mother's past to heal my future.

Support is beneficial for you while you are forging ahead on this grief from parental death journey of yours. The type of support that works best for you can be different from the type of support that works out best for others. Stay true to the support you need.

· *12* ·

Role Models in Society

*I*t might not have dawned on you yet, but there are actually a plethora of notable famous people in society who lost one or both of their parents like you did from a variety of different causes. Many of them were just a kid or young teen or adult like you when they lost their parent, and many of them lost a parent before they became the famous musician, actress, scientist, Nobel Prize Laureate, or even athlete that we all know them for today. There are literally hundreds and thousands of notable people in society who lost one or both of their parents young but grew up still giving something positive and extraordinary back to the world despite having to navigate life without one or both of their parents. Whether they contributed an inspiring song, a scientific breakthrough, a heartwarming performance from a movie they acted in, or a piece of literary work, check out this list. This is just a sample believe it or not. I have been compiling and researching names of notable society members for the last two decades to help all of you who have lost a parent young feel inspired that you too can do something positive and extraordinary with your life despite the fact that you lost one or both of your parents young. If the notable people from society on this list could do it, then so can you. Perhaps you can think of many others not on this list. Feel free to do your own research or dive deeper into researching the few that I have listed here. You might be surprised who you come across that could already be one of your favorites. Just remember that this list is compiled based on notable works from society members and those who also lost a parent at a young age. Everyone has their own path to responsibly walk and the same goes for you. The people mentioned on this list were not perfect and may have made mistakes. Let the fact that they lost their parent young and still did something extraordinary with their life inspire you, but know I am in no way saying you should make any of the same mistakes some of them may have made along the way during their individual grief journey. You and you alone are responsible for the choices and path you decide to take in your life. Check this list out with your surviving parent or caregiver.

ACTORS

- Alan Rickman—The late actor well known for being the villain in the movie *Die Hard*, as well as Professor Snape in the *Harry Potter* movie installments. His father died of lung cancer when Alan was eight years old.[1]
- Benicio del Toro—Puerto-Rican actor known for movies such as *Guardians of the Galaxy*, and *Star Wars: The Last Jedi*. His mother died when he was nine years old.[2]
- Billy Crystal—Actor known for his movies such as *America's Sweethearts*, *Analyze This*, *City Slickers*, and *When Harry Met Sally*. His father died of a heart attack when Billy was 15.[3]
- Cate Blanchett—Actress known for her movie roles in the *Lord of the Rings* franchise, *Thor: Ragnarok*, and *The Aviator*. Her father died of a sudden heart attack when she was 10 years old.[4]
- Freddie Prinze Jr.—Actor known for his movies such as *Scooby-Doo*, *Summer Catch*, and *I Know What You Did Last Summer*. His father committed suicide when Freddie was just 10 months old.[5]
- James Woods—Actor known for his movie roles in *John Q.*, *Hercules*, and *Any Given Sunday*. His father died during James's childhood.[6]
- John Goodman—Actor known for his role on the hit TV series, *Roseanne*, as well as various other movies such as *Coyote Ugly*, *The Babe*, *The Flintstones*, and *Monsters, Inc.* His father died of a heart attack when John was two years old.[7]
- Molly Shannon—Actress and comedian known for her roles on the show *Saturday Night Live*, and movies such as *The Santa Clause 2*, *How the Grinch Stole Christmas*, and *A Night at the Roxbury*. Her mother died from a car crash that Molly was also in when Molly was four years old.[8]

- Rosie O'Donnell—She is well-known as being a comedian and starring in films such as *A League of Their Own* and *Sleepless in Seattle*. Her mother died of cancer when Rosie was 10 years old.[9]
- Tim Allen—Actor and comedian known for his shows *Home Improvement* and *Last Man Standing*, as well as his movies such as *The Santa Clause, Wild Hogs,* and *Christmas with the Kranks.* His father was killed in a collision with a drunk driver when Tim was 11 years old.[10]
- Zoe Saldana—Actress known for her movie roles in *Guardians of the Galaxy,* the *Star Trek* franchise, *Avatar,* and *The Words.* Her father died in a car accident when Zoe was nine years old.[11]

ATHLETES

- Gabrielle Reece—Professional volleyball player, model, author, and Nike's first female spokeswoman. Her father died in a plane crash when she was four years old.[12]
- Ronda Rousey—Professional wrestler who is also well-known for being the first ever woman UFC fighter champion. Her father committed suicide when she was eight years old.[13]
- Travis Harmonic—Canadian professional ice hockey defense player for the Vancouver Canucks. His father died unexpectedly due to a heart attack when Travis was 10 years old. He started the D-Partner program to help other children who have lost a parent.[14]

AUTHORS AND POETS

- Amy Tan—The Chinese American *New York Times* Bestselling novelist of *The Joy Luck Club.* Her father died of a brain tumor when she was a teenager.[15]
- C. S. Lewis—Irish writer known for his Christian writings and *Chronicles of Narnia* fantasy series for children. His mother died when he was 10 years old.[16]

- Edgar Allan Poe—The dark and mysterious poet well known for *The Raven*. His mother passed away from tuberculosis when he was only three.[17]
- J. R. R. Tolkien—The famous and internationally known author of *The Hobbit* series and *The Lord of the Rings* series. His father died from rheumatic fever when Tolkien was only four, and his mother died by the time he was 12.[18]
- Joseph Conrad—Author well known for writing short stories and his novel, *Heart of Darkness*. He lost both of his parents to tuberculosis before he became a teenager.[19]
- Leo Tolstoy—Russian author known for his works, *War and Peace* and *Anna Karenina*. His mother died when he was two years old, and his father died by the time Tolstoy was nine years old.[20]
- P. L. Travers—Author of the *Mary Poppins* children's book series, which inspired Walt Disney to create the *Mary Poppins* movie on the big screen. Her father died of tuberculosis when she was only seven years old.[21]

DOCTOR

- Elizabeth Blackwell—The first woman physician in the United States. She later became well known as a leading public health activist throughout her lifetime. Her father died when she was a teenager.[22]

EDUCATOR

- Anne Sullivan—The well-respected teacher who taught Helen Keller how to read Braille and communicate, although she was deaf and blind. Anne's mother passed away from tuberculosis when Anne was eight years old.[23]

ENTREPRENEURS

- Karl Benz of Mercedes-Benz—The German mechanical engineer who built and designed the first automobile powered by an internal combustion engine. His father died when Karl was two years old.[24]
- William Boeing of the Boeing Company—He was a pioneer in airplane manufacturing and an entrepreneur. His father died of influenza when William was eight years old.[25]

HERO

- Irena Sendler—Polish social worker known for rescuing 2,500 Jewish children during World War II from the Warsaw Ghetto. Her father died of typhus when she was a child.[26]

JUDGES

- Ruth Bader Ginsburg—She was a US Supreme Court justice and the second woman to be appointed as one. Her mother died of cancer one day before Ruth's high school graduation.[27]
- Sonia Sotomayor—She made history by being the first Latina woman to become a US Supreme Court justice. Her father died before she was 10 years old.[28]

NOBEL PRIZE LAUREATES

- Elias Canetti—Bulgarian novelist and playwright who won the Nobel Prize in Literature in 1981. He is known well for his nonfiction book, *Crowds and Power*. His father died by the time Elias was eight years old.[29]
- Jean Paul Sartre—A French philosopher, novelist, and playwright who won the Nobel Prize in Literature in 1964; however,

he declined it. Sartre was one of the leaders in early existential-ism. He lost his father at an early age and was raised by his maternal grandfather, Carl Schweitzer, uncle of the well-known Albert Schweitzer.[30]

- Linus Pauling—Chemist who won not one but two Nobel Prizes; one Nobel Prize was for Chemistry in 1954, and the other was a Nobel Peace Prize in 1962. His father died when Linus was nine years old.[31]
- Mother Teresa—Known for founding the Order of the Missionaries of Charity, Mother Teresa won the Nobel Peace Prize in 1979 for all of her humanitarian work. In 2016, she was canonized (in the Roman Catholic Church, this means to be officially declared as a saint) as Saint Teresa of Calcutta. Her father died when she was eight years old.[32]
- Severo Ochoa—Biochemist and molecular biologist who received the Nobel Prize in 1959 in Physiology or Medicine alongside Arthur Kornberg, for their discovery of an enzyme in bacteria that enabled them to synthesize ribonucleic acid (RNA). His father died when Severo was seven years old.[33]
- Yasunari Kawabata—A Japanese novelist who won the Nobel Prize in Literature in 1968. He is known for writing *Thousand Cranes* and *The Sound of the Mountain*. He was orphaned at an early age.[34]

TELEVISION HOSTS

- Anderson Cooper—News Correspondent for ABC and CNN. His father died when Anderson was 11 years old during open heart surgery.[35]
- Drew Carey—Comedian known for *The Drew Carey Show* as well as the host for the show, *The Price Is Right*. His father died from a brain tumor by the time Drew was eight years old.[36]

Again, this is just a small sampling to prove to you that you are not alone, but to also inspire you that you can still lead an extraordinary life, although your parent is no longer physically here anymore.

III

RESOLUTION

The most important part of this next section is to understand and, although it might be difficult, to accept that there is no finish line to your parental death grief journey. This is not something that there is a cure for, or once you hit 30 years old, or 50 years old, that you won't be sad and miss your parent anymore. Grief, especially grief from the death of your parent young, does not work like that. I know we all wish it did so the pain would go away, but remember the quote from *WandaVision?* "What is grief, if not love persevering?" As you press on to more and more years since your parent died, this quote will really hit home for you. Every year your parent is gone is another year your love for them has persevered. They may not be physically here, but the love you have for them and the pain you feel from missing them carries you to the next year and the next. It is creating an endurance for you to know that your love for them and even their love for you never ends but continues on throughout the years and decades through life and even through death. It gets passed on to your children someday when you talk about their late grandmother or grandfather whom they sadly never got the chance to meet, but you keep their memory alive by showing your children pictures of them and by sharing memories with them. It creates a loving understanding between you and your future spouse to place certain objects of your late parents' remembrance around the home you two will share together. Your love for them will go on, and that will never change. Seasons will change in your life and the loss of your parent at a young age can create both opportunities later on down the road as well as challenges and obstacles, but the love will always remain.

· 13 ·

Different Path for Everyone

$\mathcal{F}$or some of you, support will be provided right away and from various people in your life. For others, you only had one or two secondary losses as opposed to another reader who suffered four or five after their parent's death. Maybe you started seeking counseling within a month of your parent's death, whereas another didn't start counseling for a few years. Maybe someone you know tried support groups and it worked really well for them, but when you tried them out you had a negative experience. Each individual who loses a parent at a young age is going to have a different grief path than the other. Some of you lost both parents, whereas some of you only lost one. No two paths are going to look the same. That's why it's important to make sure you have a solid support system but to also know how to grieve and cope independently in case your support group cannot be available to you all the time. It is also important to know that you might meet others who have lost a parent along your own grieving journey, but your experience will be different than theirs, and that is okay. Everyone on this journey will have a different path to take. Not everyone lost their parent at the same age, to the same cause of death, had the same type of support, or coped in the same exact way—and again that is perfectly okay. What you should be focusing on is the individual path that you are on and the choices that you should be responsibly making along the way and deciding what is the healthiest route for you to take to continue to have a bright future. The support system of people you have is there to guide you along the way—not decide the path you should take for you. Coping with parental death is a lifelong journey unique to the individual walking down this path. No two paths will be the same, so do not put more pressure on yourself and try to compare your journey to someone else's. Their path is unique just like your path is.

You also might have started going down a path in life that changes once your parent died. For some of you who lost one or both of your parents at a young age, the loss might influence you to a new life path while on your journey to becoming an adult. Perhaps this has happened to you already, and if it hasn't, maybe it will and maybe it won't.

Losing a parent young can alter the direction we decide to take as we become adults. Maybe before your parent died, you wanted to be an architect. But now, maybe you're thinking about going into nonprofit work like your late parent was doing when they passed. Or maybe you wanted to be a firefighter like your late father was, but because you lost your dad to a fire, it might make you not want to go down that path anymore. Or, if you wanted to become a teacher before your mother died of an illness, maybe now you want to become a nurse to help others who are sick from the same illness.

In society, this has happened to many notable people where the loss of their parent at a young age somehow influenced the path they took as adults. For example, P. L. Travers, the woman behind the *Mary Poppins* book series, wrote stories for children. She wrote stories about a magical nanny and about happy families that entertained children. A lot of people think that authors only write what they know, so that if Travers wrote about happy families then she must have come from one herself, right? This was simply not the case. Travers actually lost her father young to tuberculosis. We even get glimpses of what her childhood was like in the Walt Disney movie *Saving Mr. Banks*, a true story of how Walt Disney convinced Travers to make her fictional character of Mary Poppins come alive to entertain families on the big screen. A few years after *Saving Mr. Banks* was released, a sequel to the movie *Mary Poppins*, called *Mary Poppins Returns,* was made that shows another parental death scenario of the now grown-up Michael Banks having to raise his three young children as a widow after his wife passes away. In *Saving Mr. Banks*, Travers was conflicted with what Disney wanted to do for his movie because at first Disney, played by Tom Hanks, was trying to depict Mr. Banks as a bad father, when Travers was channeling saving her real father from her childhood in a fiction form. Had Travers not lost her father young, perhaps that would have altered the fictional character of Mr. Banks that she wrote in her *Mary Poppins* stories.

FEAR OF DYING THE SAME WAY
AT THE SAME AGE YOUR PARENT DID

A lot of teens and young adults who lose their parent at a young age develop a fear that they too will die the same way their parent did at the exact age they did. As hard as it may seem, you can't let this fear debilitate you as you push forward in life. Your late parent was their own individual walking their own path. Just because something happened to them at a certain age does not mean the same thing is going to happen to you. It is hard to try not to think of this because this fear is quite common among those who lost a parent at a young age.

If you lost your dad to cancer, that doesn't mean that you are going to die from cancer, too. If your mother was killed in a car accident when she was 53 years old, that doesn't mean that you are going to die in a car accident when you turn 53 years old. We all have our own path to take that will always be connected to our late parents; however, our life is ours to live, just like our parents' life was theirs to live. Although the fear is common among parentless children, we don't know when it's our time to go. Spending a lot of time worrying about something you can't control just takes away precious moments of life that you cannot get back that you could otherwise be enjoying.

FEAR OF LOSING OTHER LOVED ONES

Fear of losing your surviving loved ones will be something you will most likely experience if you haven't already. We all lost a parent at a young age before we became independent individuals. So, ask yourself, after your parent died, did you suddenly start becoming more overprotective of your little brother when before you never really worried about him? When your surviving parent says they are going on a business trip, do you suddenly worry if something bad is going to happen to them? Do you suddenly start making your family members call or text you when they get home after leaving your house late at night? This is quite common.

My Fear Regarding Losing Other Loved Ones

After my mom died, I was scared something was going to happen to my dad. Anytime he went to work, dropped us off at school, or flew on an airplane, I was terrified something bad was going to happen to him. I was worried about my brother as well. Scarily, my brother got in a really bad car accident when I was in middle school. In my head I was preparing for the worst, but thankfully he was okay. The same thing happened to my dad when I was in my early 20s. He got side swiped by a semi-truck which deeply scared me that I was going to lose him, but thankfully he was okay. I got scared again in my early 20s when my dad had to go to the hospital. When I was a teenager, my uncle fell off a chair in front of me and hit his head to where it started bleeding right away. There are so many moments after my mom died that I could share with you that I was scared or worried or stressed or had anxiety that something bad was going to happen to another family member of mine. I remember my dad told me his dad died when he was 57 years old, and by my dad telling me that number, I was terrified of my dad approaching his 57th year thinking he wouldn't make it past 57 either. Thankfully my dad is now 70 and still here.

It makes me wonder how much precious time of my life I lost worrying or being scared or anxious about something I was afraid might happen because of my mother's death.

These fears, stresses, and worries are common among parentless teens and young adults; however, they can be debilitating. If you are experiencing any of this, bring it up to your counselor or share with an adult you trust for support.

The path you are now walking is yours to decide what is the best way to proceed. It's your own unique path, and you will notice, if you haven't already, that your parent's death can and may already have altered your path in life.

· *14* ·

An Ongoing Journey

*T*his book has not been created to mislead you that there is a cure for grief from parental death. As you have probably realized by now, unfortunately there is no cure for grieving the death of your parent. This is an ongoing journey that you will take with you as the years lead you forward in your life. This book provides a load of resources, healthy coping mechanisms, helpful books, helpful movies, advice from those who lost a parent before you, and more to help you along your journey. Your journey is yours to travel alone, although there are many people and resources along the way who can help guide you. Every parental death grief journey is different and unique. Connect with others and get helpful support because it will help you over the years; reach out for those healthy supplemental and positive coping mechanisms we talked about; and grieve the way you feel is the best way for you.

Remember to take good care of yourself because I have learned the hard way that self-care is extremely important while navigating all of this. After a parental death, it seems like all of us become great caretakers of others, but we don't make time for ourselves. Promise me you will make time for yourself even if it is just five minutes each day. A bath can do wonders, a good book to snuggle under a blanket with, a feel-good movie, or just brushing your hair can make you feel a little better inside. Don't forget to get plenty of rest, eat right, and exercise. Take a step back if you need to reassess your parental death grief journey to see if you need to make any positive changes for how you are coping. As you get older your needs will change, so keep striving to live the healthiest and best life you deserve and are capable of living. Know that as you live your life, your late parent will be watching you live your life with love.

Keep revamping your grief journey as you see fit. Seeing a movie with your friends might have comforted you in your 20s, but when you hit your 40s, maybe just a hot cup of tea will do. Just remember that this is all about your upcoming journey and not about reaching a destination or a finish line of grief. By now I think after reading up to this point of this book, you realize it doesn't work like that. Your parental death grief journey will be carried with you until the day that it is your time to be reconnected with your parent once again.

DIFFERENT STAGES IN LIFE WILL BE CONNECTED

As you proceed in your life after the death of your parent, you will hit your own personal life milestones where you might be sneakily blindsided of feelings from your parent's death. These can bring a little sadness to your most joyous days, but looking at these wonderful milestones through a different lens, even though your parent is not physically here to share the joy with you, can help you through them.

My Experience of Missing out on Moments

Looking back now, I think toward the end my mother knew she wasn't going to make it, and I imagine she started thinking about all of the moments in the future she knew she was going to miss. I can't imagine how agonizing and heartbreaking that was for my mother, to know she probably wasn't going to make it to see her daughter's or even her son's life milestone moments.

When my graduation came, she wasn't there. When my wedding came, she wasn't there. When the birth of my child came, she wasn't there. She also wasn't there when I started my period, went through my first heartbreak, started and finished college, got bullied, started working, or when my first book was published. Thinking about all of the moments she wasn't here for is just going to keep making me sad and it's not going to change anything. I know deep in my heart and deep in my mother's heart that she wanted to be there for all of those special events in my life. I know she wanted to stay, so knowing that she was being forced to go out of her control, I can't imagine how hurt that made her.

Instead of focusing on all of the moments my mother wasn't here for, I try to instead focus on the moments she was here for. I am blessed for example, that I was able to spend eight Christmases with her. It could have been only five or two or none. I'm thankful that I have tons of memories shopping at the mall with her, going to Disneyland with her, and spending quality time with her doing mother-daughter stuff. I'm thankful to have memories of us singing certain songs together. I'm thankful that I'm in pictures with her and we've shared many hugs in the nine years I had with her. I'm thankful because I know sadly there are others out there, maybe even *you* reading this, who had less time with their parent than that. So, I know I should be thankful for the moments I did have with my mother and to not feel sad and only focus on the moments I didn't have with her.

GRADUATION

For the last four years of your high school career, you have worked your tail off and are ready to close this chapter of your life to open up a new one. It is a celebratory rite of passage, and everyone who means anything to you is going to be there to help you celebrate your successful milestone—everyone except your late parent that is. Your graduation day is meant to be an exciting and celebratory day, but keep in mind that this fun day might bring some sadness, jealousy, feeling alone and left out because your late parent is not there to physically help you celebrate. Seeing your friends hug their parents while you are missing yours will hit you in the feels. Again, it's a happy day and you should be proud of yourself, but the loss of your parent will float up to the surface that day whether you want it to or not, whether you think it will or not.

WEDDING DAY

The common misconception is everyone thinks you will just get over your loss as the years go by because you will magically recover from the death of your parent. People who usually say that are typically people who haven't experienced parental death yet and especially parental death at a young age. On the day of your wedding, it doesn't matter if it has been two years, 10 years, or 15 years, although it's one of the happiest days of your life, the death of your parent will come creeping back up to the surface in unexpected ways. You will serve champagne that just happened to be your mother's favorite, or seeing your late dad's twin brother will serve as a reminder that he is not there to walk you down the aisle. You will notice little things that may even turn into big things on your wedding day and upset you.

BIRTH OF YOUR CHILDREN

This day is also one of the happiest days of your life. It will be so emotionally rewarding to welcome your little one into the world, but then again it can also spark a little sadness of what you're missing out on—having your late parent there to meet your child, their grandchild. It will sting while at the same time you are happy bonding with your new little one. It will also make you realize how much of your life has moved on past the death of your parent because that probably means they have missed so much at this point. Then you might start thinking of the future as your little one grows up, your late parent won't see them start school, play a sport, or be all together for the holidays.

OTHER CLOSE PERSONAL DEATHS

As you are moving on through the years still navigating the death of your parent, remember that with life comes death, and your parent's death might not be the only death you have a close encounter with. Eventually you will also lose your surviving parent or guardian, you could lose a sibling or friend, grandparents, and more. With each death, specks of your late parent's death will again come to the surface. Your parent's death has taught you a lot so far and, perhaps in some ways, has even prepared you for other deaths, but it still won't be easy.

CELEBRATORY DAYS

Retirement, your kids' graduations, getting a promotion at work, losing 40 pounds, winning a contest, watching your kids grow up, winning an award, graduating college or grad school—these will circle back to the death of your parent as well. Again, these are celebratory moments meant for happiness and joy, but they are also reminders that your late parent could not be here to help you celebrate.

HARD SCARY DAYS

Job loss, divorce, loss of relationship, an accident that now caused a permanent injury, a fight with a friend, a speeding ticket—all of these can bring up feelings of loss and what ifs that your late parent is not here anymore for you to pick up the phone and call them for advice. Everyone has bad days every now and then, but when you lose a parent at a young age, hard days in the future can connect to the hardest day of your past.

My Preserving Memories Advice for You

I notice that as I am getting older, it's getting a little harder to remember certain things about my mother. I now don't really remember the sound of her voice as well as I did when she recently passed away. Sadly, we only have one family video with her in it and it's on VHS. She only spoke for about three minutes. We used to own a family deli right before she died, and we were at the deli where the filming took place. She was sick, and you could tell her health was declining. That video is the only connection I have left to her voice. Looking back, I don't remember ever cooking with my mother, or my mother cooking. I don't remember her cleaning, and I vaguely can see her laughing and smiling in my memories. Every now and then I will get a whiff of someone's perfume, and it will trigger her memory if it was similar to what she used to wear, but a lot of these memories, I am learning fade through time. If your loss is new, I highly recommend preserving whatever you can right away so when the loss is almost three decades later for you,

you can hang on to more memories than I could. I was so young, but back then there weren't cell phones to just take out of your pocket and start recording like there are today. You had to take out your video camera. Same with pictures; people took less pictures when I was a kid compared with you as a teen or young adult now. Preserve what memories you can because one day you might not be able to remember what your late mother's voice sounded like, or remember your late father's laugh, and more. I think as we get older, because we lost our parents at such a young age, it's just going to continue to get more challenging to remember things we basically took for granted inadvertently when they were alive.

Future events are coming your way to be celebrated, just know and be prepared that the death of your parent will never just go away out of your mind wholeheartedly. Their death will always linger, and certain events can trigger the pain from your past. This is where it can benefit you to have those supplementary go-to methods lined up that we talked about for those just-in-case grief trigger moments. Always have a coloring book and markers on hand; it doesn't matter if you are 15 or 45, coloring is a form of art therapy. Have your favorite grief go-to book sitting next to your bed in case you need it and have a few parental death movies on standby. Do what you need to do for you as long as it is healthy and positive, and you are not harming yourself or anyone else. And just something to think about, as you get older, your supplementary methods might change with age. Maybe swimming helped you cope when you were in your early 20s, but maybe yoga helps you now in your late 30s. Don't be afraid to be open to adjusting or updating your coping methods.

Parting Advice from Those Who Lost a Parent

$\mathcal{A}$s you have realized by now, especially after reading this book, you are definitely not alone in navigating the death of your parent at a young age. Although this might not make you feel any better, and it clearly won't bring your late parent back, at least you know that you are not the only one out there going through this. The following words are from others before you who are various ages now, but all lost their parent young. Perhaps you can relate to their words of advice, or perhaps on the following pages you can even relate to how their parent died. Reading others' experiences can help give you context into your own experience. The takeaway is that you are not alone, you never have been, and you will never be alone moving forward.

"Take a deep breath, cry, and keep moving forward. Just take the next step, then the next. And cry while you are moving. Take time to rest. Move through one day at a time, and don't give up. Have fun when you can, and accept the support and love of people around you. It's hard because your friends just don't know what to do. I had many well-meaning people say really hurtful things. Give others grace as they clumsily try to pour healing into your life. They are coming from a place of inexperience."—Liz, lost her father to colon cancer[1]

"The advice I have is that you have to keep going, but you don't have to let go. People will try to make you feel like you have to let go of them, that you shouldn't be sad after a certain period of time. Remembering your parent is your strength. Remembering the lessons they taught you is your strength, even if those lessons make you cry. Remembering the time you had with them is their legacy."—Sharon, lost her father to complications of a rare blood disorder called catastrophic antiphospholipid syndrome[2]

"My advice to a kid who just lost a parent would be that it sucks, the pain doesn't go away, but you will feel them with you a lot more than you think. You get to have the heartwarming experience of appreciating them at such a young age and you will become a better person because of it. People will always be awkward when they find out your parents are dead as long as they have never lost a parent."—Taylor, lost her mother to leukemia and her father to a heart attack[3]

"This really hurts right now, and your life will never be the same. But hopefully there are people in your life who care about you and are willing to help you get through this mourning period and you will get a new balance back in your new reality. As bad as this is, it will get better. Your parent would want you to be happy again one day, so please be open to that once you get through the pain. Whatever faith you practice, embrace that part that gives you hope in the hereafter. If you don't believe in a hereafter that's okay, but find something that completes the circle for you."—Thad, lost his mother to breast cancer[4]

"Realize that it is out of your control and to always look forward."—Chase, lost his father to suicide[5]

"Grieve, mourn, you don't have to be strong, ask for help; if you can't find support, seek it out."—Nicci, lost her father to sudden and unexpected cardiac arrest[6]

"[Don't] keep the pain inside and suffer alone. Tell someone you trust that you feel like you need help. It is much more acceptable now than when I was a child to seek help."—Georgianne, lost her father to a hole in his heart from rheumatic fever[7]

"For me, [offering advice] feels like risky territory because my experience was my own and it's 20+ years later and the world is much different. But, the realizations (even some that I didn't figure out until recent years) I wish I had known earlier are:

Figure 15.1. Losing one or both of your parents young is a difficult situation to navigate. Although you might have some really hard days up ahead, know that the love for your late parents will always remain and will help you face each day moving forward without them. Illustration by Kate Haberer

"Feelings didn't and still don't show up when I expect them to, and very rarely when it was convenient. For example:

- I had fun at my mom's funeral and the party afterward seeing family and friends.
- I cried during math class a month later—like really hard with snot and everything.
- I felt proud and excited at my wedding and graduation—I wished my mom was there but it made me want to talk about her and the feelings I expected at those milestones weren't there.
- I felt immense sorrow and cried (again hard and ugly) when the 49ers made it to Super Bowl two years ago because my mom would have been so excited. I was so completely caught off guard that it took me a few minutes to figure out why it was happening.
- I was watching a movie called *Life As a House* on a first date in college and I had to leave before the waterworks came. I don't think another date happened . . . but that may not have been about just the crying?
- My father passed away a year ago. I cried the day he died and I have carried feelings of anger since.
- I would be able to laugh about 'yo mama' jokes because I had the only comeback that would shut them up and I loved it.

"I wish I had allowed my feelings to happen and not been too self-conscious to talk about them. I wish I had been able to override embarrassment and other people's expectations and say:

- I am sad because my mom died.
- Can I talk to you about this feeling?
- Can you just hang out while I work through this?
- Can you go away while I work through this?
- I don't want your advice.
- I don't want to be comforted.
- Telling me she is in a better place is incredibly insulting because where is there a place that's better than us being together?
- Just tell me 'that sucks' and hang out with me.

"The grief and impacts of losing my mom are still happening 20-something years later. Sadness hits now—sometimes it passes, sometimes it leads me to a happy memory, and sometimes it stops everything that is going on and I have to talk or cry or exercise it out. I say that it has evolved for me and has informed my life and who I am, it is always there and I will always miss my person and will always want them back. But it is not gone and I don't think it ever will."

"I saw an illustration once that, in the first panel showed a big bookshelf with only one book called 'Grief' to explain how it feels right away. In the second panel it is the same bookshelf and 'Grief' is still there, but now the shelf is full of other books. This summed my experience up perfectly. It's still on my shelf, but not the only book I have to go to.

"For better and for worse, this experience shaped who I am now and I am still trying to figure out the full impact of what this means. It is hard to focus on the positive ways but I feel like I am a more caring, motivated, and open person because of my experience. And of course, the negatives. Anxiety around being a caretaker, fixing things for family, and losing people. Guilt around having more years with my mom than my brother and feeling the need to somehow make it up to him. Shame around not living up to the dream my mom had for her own life and was not able to complete.

"I have a memory from early on that helps me explain that last bit. My mom made baked potatoes one evening for our family. Three of the baked potatoes turned out fine but one exploded. She took the exploded potato and gave us the non-exploded potato. Now, I don't really like baked potatoes—I just see them as a vehicle for chili and cheese, but this story exemplifies who my mom was and what I need to live up to and carry on—selflessness, compassion, kindness, and self-sacrifice above all. It has taken on a life of its own and I feel contact shame if I do not live up to this at every opportunity. So much so that I tattooed a pelican with a bleeding chest (a symbol of selflessness) on my arm as a reminder of who I feel I need to be. This has caused more difficulty in my life than I realized that I have tried so hard to live my mom's life that I don't really know what is me.

"I wish I had been more open to therapy earlier on and that it had been more about helping me prepare for my life as an adult."—Travis, lost his mother to cervical cancer[8]

"It's okay to grieve. Everything happens for a reason whether it's good or bad. You will become who you were meant to be, and your parent passing is the reason it will happen. It's okay to fantasize about who they were and what role they would have played in your life. Embrace any and all who give you positive reinforcement. If you find that your mental stability is wavering, seek help. It's okay."—Dani R., lost her mother to non-Hodgkin lymphoma[9]

"Don't shut yourself in. Find your support and your coping mechanism. I am always open to talk, although I am a stranger. The best thing I found when I was going through it was the support of someone who understood what I was going through. Losing a parent is a very unique experience, terrible but unique in the sense not everyone will understand. Most people won't. But it's so nice to have at least one person you can talk to and ask questions or advice to. There are definitely bad ways to cope anything with substances being one. But otherwise don't lose yourself in grief. Find time for yourself and for the things you love."—Lola, lost her father to pneumonia and neuroendocrine cancer[10]

"Don't let the depression get to you. I almost lost my life over it. The pain will get better, it won't go away but it gets easier. I felt like I would never feel the same again but, time really does heal."—Reaghan, lost her father to cardiac arrest[11]

"[It is helpful] to have a supportive extended family and a close circle of friends. Don't be afraid to ask for help. Grieving isn't a sign of weakness. There is no timetable as to say you will feel better in time (definitely not true). Maybe find a supportive teacher or counselor."—Debbie, lost her father to pancreatic cancer[12]

"Your feelings are valid. If you've just lost a parent or like me, you're suffering from late grief, it's absolutely okay. There will be bad days when you miss them like crazy and you will do anything just to see them again or hear their voice again and that is absolutely fine. If you have memories, hold on to them as closely as you can for as long as you can. But don't feel guilty for having good days, don't feel guilty for laughing and smiling because I'm sure your parents would love to see you smile again. Don't feel guilty for doing something for the first time without them, it will be hard, very hard but you'll get through it. I may not know you personally, but I know that everyone reading this is strong.

"And remember, seeking help if/when you need it is a massive step forward. It doesn't make you weak, it makes you incredibly brave. And I'm proud of you for that.

"Your teenage years can be difficult and at times you do just want your mum and or dad with you to tell you that everything is going to be okay and that you are going to be okay. It will be tough not having them there to say that or to support you when things go bad. But you have to remind yourself that things will be okay. You will be okay. Maybe not straight away, but one day you'll wake up and realise that, yeah you are okay.

"Although my family isn't very religious, I was always told that my mum was in heaven in the sky looking down on me, protecting me, helping me along the way without me realising it. And although sometimes I feel dumb for still believing that it has helped me feel close to her and it has helped me feel like she is still here, still close to me.

"As I previously said I am a Marvel fan so the *WandaVision* quote 'what is grief, if not love persevering' has helped me remember that the way I feel is proof that my mum is never really gone. I may not remember her, and I may not know much about her but I know she means a lot to me, I know that she is still watching over me and looking out for me. And I still and always will love her.

"You are incredibly strong and over time things will start to get a bit better. Don't ever feel guilty for missing them or grieving them, even if people have moved on or tell you to move on, take it one step at a time at your pace. Losing a parent is hard, very hard. And you are so brave. No one expects you to move on overnight.

"If you have memories, hold on to them. If you have photos and videos, keep them safe and backed up on a hard drive so you never run the risk of losing them. If you have items of clothing or jewelry, look after them and keep them safe. Wear them if you want. Since about 16 I've always worn the ring that my dad gave to mum after I was born (a 'pushing present') and it has helped me feel closer to her.

"If you know any of the songs they liked or the films or TV shows they liked, watch them, and don't feel guilty for doing it without them or doing traditions without them. Don't feel guilty for celebrating certain holidays or birthdays without them. They'd want you to be happy."—Jessica, lost her mother to cervical cancer[13]

MY PARTING ADVICE FOR YOU

You are the author of your own story. Your late parent would not want their death to break your life. They would want you to live your life to the fullest and make something wonderful out of it. There is no doubt that their loss will stay with you forever as you journey on to adulthood, but your parent would not want their death to debilitate your life.

What may work for one teen or young adult grieving might be different for another teen or young adult. While you are embarking on your grief journey, you need to remember to stay true to who you are and know that you might need something different than another peer who lost their parent. Everyone grieves differently, and this is something you will learn and see more and more of while you are maturing with learning how to navigate your grief. In the end, you and only you can make the choice on what grieving method is best for you. And with saying that comes responsibility as well. Just like Peter Parker, also known as Spider-Man, was told by his Uncle Ben, with great power comes great responsibility. You have the power to walk along the grief path that you choose. However, if you choose to walk down a negative path, then you are choosing to accept the consequences that come with them. Choose wisely, as your future depends on the choices you make now. Peter Parker struggled with learning a few of these lessons. Learn from him and others who have walked down this grief path before you.

I am sending you a virtual hug. If you ever feel alone, know that in your heart I am always here for you.

Appendix A

Helpful Books

Remember to check with your parent or guardian first before reading to make sure the overall book is something they want you reading because there might be other life discussions mentioned in these books.

- *American Girl: Meet Marie-Grace* by Sarah Buckey (Fiction)
- *Beauty and the Beast: Lost in a Book* by Jennifer Donnelly (Fiction)
- *The Beginning of After* by Jennifer Castle (Fiction)
- *The Boy in the Black Suit* by Jason Reynolds (Fiction)
- *The Care and Feeding of a Pet Black Hole* by Michelle Cuevas (Fiction)
- *Coco* a Disney Pixar Little Golden Book (Fiction)
- *Daughters without Dads* by Lois Mowday Rabey (Nonfiction)
- *David Copperfield* by Charles Dickens (Fiction)
- *The Dead Moms Club* by Kate Spencer (Memoir)
- *Extremely Loud and Incredibly Close* by Jonathan Safran Foer (Fiction)
- *Father Fiction* by Donald Miller (Nonfiction)
- *Father Loss* by Neil Chethik (Nonfiction)
- *The Fatherless Daughter Project* by Denna D. Babul, RN, and Karin L. Smithson, PhD (Nonfiction)
- *Fatherless Daughters* by Pamela Thomas (Nonfiction)
- *Fatherless Women* by Clea Simon (Nonfiction)
- *Grief Is Like a Snowflake* by Julia Cook (Fiction)
- *The Grieving Teen* by Helen Fitzgerald (Nonfiction)
- *H Is for Hawk* by Helen Macdonald (Nonfiction)
- *Harry Potter and the Chamber of Secrets* by J. K. Rowling (Fiction)

- *Harry Potter and the Deathly Hallows* by J. K. Rowling (Fiction)
- *Harry Potter and the Goblet of Fire* by J. K. Rowling (Fiction)
- *Harry Potter and the Half-Blood Prince* by J. K. Rowling (Fiction)
- *Harry Potter and the Order of the Phoenix* by J. K. Rowling (Fiction)
- *Harry Potter and the Prisoner of Azkaban* by J. K. Rowling (Fiction)
- *Harry Potter and the Sorcerer's Stone* by J. K. Rowling (Fiction)
- *Healing Your Grieving Heart for Teens: 100 Practical Ideas* by Alan D. Wolfelt, PhD (Nonfiction)
- *Her Mother's Face* by Roddy Doyle (Fiction)
- *How to Be Brave* by E. Katherine Kottaras (Fiction)
- *How to Save a Life* by Sara Zarr (Fiction)
- *I Kill Giants* by Joe Kelly and J. M. Ken Niimura (Fiction)
- *I'll Always Be with You* by Violetta Armour (Fiction)
- *In Her Shoes* by Jennifer Weiner (Fiction)
- *Kissing in America* by Margo Rabb (Fiction)
- *Land of Stories: Beyond the Kingdoms* by Chris Colfer (Fiction)
- *Land of Stories: The Enchantress Returns* by Chris Colfer (Fiction)
- *Land of Stories: The Wishing Spell* by Chris Colfer (Fiction)
- *Letters from Motherless Daughters* by Hope Edelman (Nonfiction)
- *The Long Goodbye* by Meghan O'Rourke (Memoir)
- *Longing for Dad: Father Loss and Its Impact* by Beth M. Erickson, PhD (Nonfiction)
- *Lost Fathers: How Women Can Heal from Adolescent Father Loss* by Laraine Herring (Nonfiction)
- *Love and Gelato* by Jenna Evans Welch (Fiction)
- *The Magic Mountain* by Thomas Mann (Fiction)
- *Missing Mom* by Joyce Carol Oates (Fiction)
- *Missing Mommy* by Rebecca Cobb (Fiction)
- *A Monster Calls* by Patrick Ness (Fiction)
- *Motherless Daughters* by Hope Edelman (Nonfiction)
- *Motherless Mothers* by Hope Edelman (Nonfiction)
- *Nancy Drew* series by Carolyn Keene (Fiction)
- *Oliver Twist* by Charles Dickens (Fiction)
- *On Grieving the Death of a Father* by Harold Ivan Smith (Nonfiction)

- *The Paris Wife* by Paula McLain (Fiction)
- *The Phantom of the Opera* by Gaston Leroux (Fiction)
- *Ready Player One* by Ernest Cline (Fiction)
- *Remembering Mama* by Dara Dokas (Fiction)
- *The Scar* by Charlotte Moundlic (Fiction)
- *The Secret Garden* by Frances Hodgson Burnett (Fiction)
- *The Survival Kit* by Donna Freitas (Fiction)
- *A Teen Girl's Guide to Grief: After the Loss of Her Mother* by Wendy Young, LMSW, BCD (Nonfiction)
- *A Teen Guy's Guide to Grief: After the Loss of His Father* by Wendy Young, LMSW, BCD (Nonfiction)
- *Tiger Eyes* by Judy Blume (Fiction)
- *The Truth about Forever* by Sarah Dessen (Fiction)
- *We Are Okay* by Nina LaCour (Fiction)
- *What to Do When I Am Gone: A Mother's Wisdom to Her Daughter* by Suzy Hopkins and Hallie Bateman (Graphic Novel/Self-Help)
- *When Kids and Teens Grieve: Remembering a Parent* by Kidlutions.com (Nonfiction)
- *When Your Father Dies* by Dave Veerman and Bruce Barton (Nonfiction)
- *You Are Not Alone* by Lynne B. Hughes (Nonfiction)

Appendix B

Helpful Movies

Remember to check with your parent or guardian first before watching to make sure the overall movie is something they want you watching because there might be other life discussions mentioned in these movies.

- *27 Dresses*. Comedy/romance, 2008. 111 minutes.
- *50 First Dates*. Comedy/drama/romance, 2004. 99 minutes.
- *Aladdin*. Animation/adventure/comedy/family/fantasy/musical/romance, 1992. 90 minutes.
- *Always Be My Maybe*. Comedy/romance, 2019. 101 minutes.
- *The Amazing Spider-man*. Action/adventure/fantasy/sci-fi, 2012. 136 minutes.
- *The Amazing Spider-man 2*. Action/adventure/fantasy/sci-fi, 2014. 142 minutes.
- *Angels in the Outfield*. Comedy/family/fantasy/sport, 1994. 102 minutes.
- *Ant-Man*. Action/adventure/comedy/sci-fi, 2015. 117 minutes.
- *Armageddon*. Action/adventure/sci-fi/thriller, 1998. 151 minutes.
- *Atlantis: The Lost Empire*. Animation/action/adventure/family/fantasy/sci-fi, 2001. 95 minutes.
- *Avatar*. Action/adventure/fantasy/sci-fi, 2009. 162 minutes.
- *Avengers: Endgame*. Action/adventure/drama/sci-fi, 2019. 181 minutes.
- *Avengers: Infinity War*. Action/adventure/sci-fi, 2018. 149 minutes.
- *Bambi*. Animation/drama/family, 1942. 70 minutes.
- *Batman Begins*. Action/adventure, 2005. 140 minutes.

- *Batman vs Superman: Dawn of Justice.* Action/adventure/sci-fi, 2016. 152 minutes.
- *Beauty and the Beast.* Animation/family/fantasy/musical/romance, 1991. 84 minutes.
- *Black Panther.* Action/adventure/sci-fi, 2018. 134 minutes.
- *The Blind Side.* Biography/drama/sport, 2009. 129 minutes.
- *The Boys Are Back.* Drama, 2009. 104 minutes.
- *Burlesque.* Drama/music, 2010. 119 minutes.
- *Captain America: Civil War.* Action/adventure/sci-fi, 2016. 147 minutes.
- *Captain America: The First Avenger.* Action/adventure/sci-fi, 2011. 124 minutes.
- *Casper.* Comedy/family/fantasy, 1995. 100 minutes.
- *The Christmas Chronicles.* Adventure/comedy/family/fantasy, 2018. 104 minutes.
- *Christopher Robin.* Animation/adventure/comedy/drama/family/fantasy/musical, 2018. 104 minutes.
- *Cloudy with a Chance of Meatballs.* Animation/adventure/comedy/drama/family/fantasy/sci-fi, 2009. 90 minutes.
- *The Club.* Documentary, 2014. 75 minutes.
- *Coco.* Animation/adventure/comedy/family/fantasy/music/mystery, 2017. 105 minutes.
- *Corrina, Corrina.* Comedy/drama/romance, 1994. 115 minutes.
- *Creed.* Drama/sport, 2015. 133 minutes.
- *Dan in Real Life.* Comedy/drama/romance, 2007. 98 minutes.
- *Daredevil.* Action/crime, 2003. 103 minutes.
- *Disturbia.* Crime/drama/mystery/thriller, 2007. 105 minutes.
- *Dumbo.* Adventure/family/fantasy, 2019. 112 minutes.
- *Elektra.* Action/adventure/crime/fantasy, 2005. 97 minutes.
- *Ella Enchanted.* Comedy/family/fantasy/romance, 2004. 96 minutes.
- *Extremely Loud and Incredibly Close.* Adventure/drama/mystery, 2011. 129 minutes.
- *Fantastic Beasts and Where to Find Them.* Adventure/family/fantasy, 2016. 132 minutes.
- *Fantastic Beasts: The Crimes of Grindelwald.* Adventure/family/fantasy, 2018. 134 minutes.
- *Fantastic Four.* Action/adventure/fantasy/sci-fi, 2005. 106 minutes.

- *Finding Nemo.* Animation/adventure/comedy/family, 2003. 100 minutes.
- *Fly Away Home.* Adventure/drama/family, 1996. 107 minutes.
- *Forrest Gump.* Drama/romance, 1994. 142 minutes.
- *Freaky Friday.* Comedy/family/fantasy/music/romance, 2003. 97 minutes.
- *Frequency.* Crime/drama/mystery/sci-fi/thriller, 2000. 118 minutes.
- *Frozen.* Animation/adventure/comedy/family/fantasy/musical, 2013. 102 minutes.
- *Garden State.* Comedy/drama/romance, 2004. 102 minutes.
- *Ghost of Girlfriends Past.* Comedy/fantasy/romance, 2009. 100 minutes.
- *Godzilla.* Action/adventure/sci-fi/thriller, 2014. 123 minutes.
- *Gone with the Wind.* Drama/history/romance/war, 1939. 238 minutes.
- *The Good Dinosaur.* Animation/adventure/comedy/drama/family/fantasy, 2015. 93 minutes.
- *Goosebumps.* Adventure/comedy/family/fantasy/horror, 2015. 103 minutes.
- *The Great Mouse Detective.* Animation/adventure/family/musical/mystery, 1986. 74 minutes.
- *The Greatest Showman.* Biography/drama/musical, 2017. 105 minutes.
- *Guardians of the Galaxy.* Action/adventure/comedy/sci-fi, 2014. 121 minutes.
- *Hansel and Gretel: Witch Hunters.* Action/fantasy/horror, 2013. 88 minutes.
- *Harry Potter and the Chamber of Secrets.* Adventure/family/fantasy/mystery, 2002. 161 minutes.
- *Harry Potter and the Deathly Hallows: Part 1.* Adventure/fantasy/mystery, 2010. 146 minutes.
- *Harry Potter and the Deathly Hallows: Part 2.* Adventure/drama/fantasy/mystery, 2011. 130 minutes.
- *Harry Potter and the Goblet of Fire.* Adventure/family/fantasy/mystery, 2005. 157 minutes.
- *Harry Potter and the Half-Blood Prince.* Action/adventure/family/fantasy/mystery, 2009. 153 minutes.

- *Harry Potter and the Order of the Phoenix.* Action/adventure/family/fantasy/mystery, 2007. 138 minutes.
- *Harry Potter and the Prisoner of Azkaban.* Adventure/family/fantasy/mystery, 2004. 142 minutes.
- *Harry Potter and the Sorcerer's Stone.* Adventure/family/fantasy, 2001. 152 minutes.
- *Hidden Figures.* Biography/drama/history, 2016. 127 minutes.
- *The Holiday.* Comedy/romance, 2006. 136 minutes.
- *Hook.* Adventure/comedy/family/fantasy, 1991. 142 minutes.
- *Hotel Transylvania.* Animation/adventure/comedy/family/fantasy/horror/romance, 2012. 91 minutes.
- *Hotel Transylvania 2.* Animation/action/adventure/comedy/family/fantasy/horror/romance, 2015. 89 minutes.
- *Hotel Transylvania 3: Summer Vacation.* Animation/adventure/comedy/family/fantasy/horror/romance, 2018. 97 minutes.
- *How to Train Your Dragon.* Animation/action/adventure/drama/family/fantasy, 2010. 98 minutes.
- *The Hundred-Foot Journey.* Comedy/drama, 2014. 122 minutes.
- *I Can Only Imagine.* Biography/drama/family/music, 2018. 110 minutes.
- *I Kill Giants.* Drama/fantasy/thriller, 2017. 106 minutes.
- *In Her Shoes.* Comedy/drama/romance, 2005. 130 minutes.
- *The Incredible Hulk.* Action/adventure/sci-fi, 2008. 112 minutes.
- *Incredibles 2.* Animation/action/adventure/comedy/family/sci-fi, 2018. 118 minutes.
- *Independence Day.* Action/adventure/sci-fi, 1996. 145 minutes.
- *Indiana Jones and the Last Crusade.* Action/adventure, 1989. 127 minutes.
- *Interstellar.* Adventure/drama/sci-fi, 2014. 169 minutes.
- *Iron Man.* Action/adventure/sci-fi, 2008. 126 minutes.
- *The Italian Job.* Action/crime/thriller, 2003. 111 minutes.
- *It's a Wonderful Life.* Drama/family/fantasy, 1946. 130 minutes.
- *Jack Frost.* Comedy/drama/family/fantasy, 1998. 101 minutes.
- *Johnny Tsunami.* Drama/family/sport, 1999. 88 minutes.
- *The Judge.* Crime/drama, 2014. 141 minutes.
- *Justice League.* Action/adventure/fantasy/sci-fi, 2017. 120 minutes.
- *Kick-Ass.* Action/comedy/crime, 2010. 117 minutes.

- *The Kid.* Comedy/family/fantasy, 2000. 104 minutes.
- *The Land Before Time.* Animation/adventure/drama/family, 1988. 69 minutes.
- *Lara Croft Tomb Raider: The Cradle of Life.* Action/adventure/fantasy, 2003. 117 minutes.
- *Lara Croft: Tomb Raider.* Action/adventure/fantasy/thriller, 2001. 100 minutes.
- *Letters to Juliet.* Adventure/comedy/drama/romance, 2010. 105 minutes.
- *Lift Me Up.* Family, 2015. 108 minutes.
- *Lilo and Stitch.* Animation/adventure/comedy/drama/family/fantasy/sci-fi, 2002. 92 minutes.
- *The Lion King.* Animation/adventure/drama/family/musical, 1994. 88 minutes.
- *The Lord of the Rings: The Fellowship of the Rings.* Action/adventure/drama/fantasy, 2001. 178 minutes.
- *Louder than Bombs.* Drama, 2015. 109 minutes.
- *Love Actually.* Comedy/drama/romance, 2003. 135 minutes.
- *Man of Steel.* Action/adventure/sci-fi, 2013. 143 minutes.
- *Manchester by the Sea.* Drama, 2016. 137 minutes.
- *Mary Poppins Returns.* Comedy/family/fantasy/musical, 2018. 130 minutes.
- *A Mom for Christmas.* Fantasy/comedy/family, 1990. 96 minutes.
- *A Monster Calls.* Adventure/drama/family/fantasy, 2016. 108 minutes.
- *Muppet Treasure Island.* Action/adventure/comedy/family/musical/romance, 1996. 99 minutes.
- *My Girl.* Comedy/drama/family/romance, 1991. 102 minutes.
- *The Neverending Story.* Adventure/drama/family/fantasy, 1984. 102 minutes.
- *Newsies.* Drama/family/history/musical, 1992. 121 minutes.
- *No Reservations.* Comedy/drama/romance, 2007. 104 minutes.
- *Noelle.* Adventure/comedy/family/fantasy/romance, 2019. 100 minutes.
- *The Notebook.* Drama/romance, 2004. 123 minutes.
- *Now and Then.* Comedy/drama/romance, 1995. 100 minutes.
- *Now You See Me.* Crime/mystery/thriller, 2013. 115 minutes.

- *Olympus Has Fallen.* Action/thriller, 2013. 119 minutes.
- *Onward.* Animation/adventure/comedy/family/fantasy, 2020. 102 minutes.
- *Pacific Rim Uprising.* Action/adventure/sci-fi, 2018. 111 minutes.
- *Peter Pan.* Animation/adventure/family/fantasy/musical, 1953. 77 minutes.
- *Peter Rabbit 2: The Runaway.* Animation/adventure/comedy/family/fantasy, 2021. 93 minutes.
- *Peter Rabbit.* Animation/adventure/comedy/family/fantasy, 2018. 95 minutes.
- *The Phantom of the Opera.* Drama/musical/romance/thriller, 2004. 143 minutes.
- *Pirates of the Caribbean: The Curse of the Black Pearl.* Action/adventure/fantasy, 2003. 143 minutes.
- *Practical Magic.* Comedy/drama/fantasy/romance, 1998. 104 minutes.
- *The Princess and the Frog.* Animation/adventure/comedy/family/fantasy/musical/romance, 2009. 97 minutes.
- *The Princess Diaries.* Comedy/family/romance, 2001. 115 minutes.
- *Ratatouille.* Animation/adventure/comedy/family/fantasy, 2007. 111 minutes.
- *Ready Player One.* Action/adventure/sci-fi, 2018. 140 minutes.
- *Real Steel.* Action/drama/sci-fi/sport, 2011. 127 minutes.
- *Remember the Titans.* Biography/drama/sport, 2000. 113 minutes.
- *Robin Hood.* Action/adventure/drama/history, 2010. 140 minutes.
- *Rogue One: A Star Wars Story.* Action/adventure/sci-fi, 2016. 133 minutes.
- *Rugrats in Paris.* Animation/adventure/comedy/family/romance, 2000. 78 minutes.
- *Saving Mr. Banks.* Biography/comedy/drama, 2013. 125 minutes.
- *Signs.* Drama/mystery/sci-fi/thriller, 2002. 106 minutes.
- *Simply Irresistible.* Comedy/drama/fantasy/romance, 1999. 96 minutes.

- *The Sisterhood of the Traveling Pants.* Comedy/drama/romance, 2005. 119 minutes.
- *Sleepless in Seattle.* Comedy/drama/romance, 1993. 105 minutes.
- *Snow White and the Huntsman.* Action/adventure/drama/fantasy, 2012. 127 minutes.
- *Southpaw.* Action/drama/sport, 2015. 124 minutes.
- *Star Trek.* Action/adventure/sci-fi, 2009. 127 minutes.
- *Stuart Little 2.* Animation/adventure, 2002. 77 minutes.
- *Surf's Up.* Animation/adventure/comedy/family/sport, 2007. 85 minutes.
- *The Tale of Despereaux.* Animation/adventure/comedy/family/fantasy, 2008. 93 minutes.
- *Tarzan.* Animation/adventure/comedy/family, 1999. 88 minutes.
- *Thor: Ragnarok.* Action/adventure/comedy/fantasy/sci-fi, 2017. 130 minutes.
- *Thor: The Dark World.* Action/adventure/fantasy, 2013. 112 minutes
- *Tomb Raider.* Action/adventure/fantasy/thriller, 2018. 119 minutes.
- *Top Gun.* Action/drama, 1986. 110 minutes.
- *Transformers: Age of Extinction.* Action/adventure/sci-fi, 2014. 165 minutes.
- *Tron: Legacy.* Action/adventure/sci-fi, 2010. 125 minutes.
- *Twister.* Action/adventure/thriller, 1996. 113 minutes.
- *We Bought a Zoo.* Comedy/drama/family, 2011. 124 minutes.
- *The Wedding Planner.* Comedy/romance, 2001. 103 minutes.
- *You've Got Mail.* Comedy/drama/romance, 1998. 119 minutes.

Notes

CHAPTER 1

1. Denise Winterman, "Children of the Great War." *BBC News Magazine.* http://news.bbc.co.uk/2/hi/uk_news/magazine/7082625.stm, accessed August 17, 2021.

2. "Widows and Orphans," *Encyclopedia.com.* https://www.encyclopedia.com/defense/energy-government-and-defense-magazines/widows-and-orphans, accessed August 17, 2021.

3. United for the Fallen, "Mission Statement," https://theunitedforthefallen.com/, accessed August 17, 2021.

4. Wayne Drash, "'Daddy's in Heaven': Rig Victims' Families Share Memories, Mementos." *CNN.com,* August 2010. http://www.cnn.com/2010/US/07/29/rig.victim.families/index.html, accessed August 17, 2021.

5. Avert, "Children, HIV, and AIDS." https://www.avert.org/professionals/hiv-social-issues/key-affected-populations/children, accessed August 17, 2021.

6. National Center for Biotechnology Information and US National Library of Medicine, "Improving Emotional Health and Self-Esteem of Malaysian Adolescents Living in Orphanages through Life Skills Education Program: A Multi-Centre Randomized Control Trial." *NCBI,* December 26, 2019. https://www.ncbi.nlm.nih.gov/pmc/articles/PMC6932807/, accessed August 17, 2021.

7. "Households with Kids Who Lost Parents in Great East Japan Quake and Tsunami Face Poverty," *The Mainichi,* December 12, 2020. https://mainichi.jp/english/articles/20201212/p2a/00m/0na/016000c, accessed August 17, 2021.

8. Rebecca Clifford, "Families after the Holocaust: Between the Archives and Oral History." *Oral History* 46, no. 1 (2018): 4 –54. https://www.jstor.org/stable/44993455 accessed, August 17, 2021.

9. "Children Who Lose a Parent to Suicide More Likely to Die the Same Way," *Johns Hopkins Medicine*, April 21, 2010. https://www.hopkinsmedicine.org/news/media/releases/children_who_lose_a_parent_to_suicide_more_likely_to_die_the_same_way, accessed August 17, 2021.

10. Robert Preidt, "1.5 Million Kids Worldwide Lost Parent or Other Caregiver to COVID-19." *US NEWS*, July 2021. https://www.usnews.com/news/health-news/articles/2021-07-21/15-million-kids-worldwide-lost-parent-or-other-caregiver-to-covid-19, accessed August 17, 2021.

11. Edward Tabor Linenthal, "Oklahoma City Bombing," in Oklahoma Historical Society, *The Encyclopedia of Oklahoma History and Culture*. https://www.okhistory.org/publications/enc/entry.php?entry=OK026, accessed August 17, 2021.

12. Debbie Elliott, "In Haiti, Quake's Orphans Long for a Home." *NPR*, March 9, 2010. https://www.npr.org/templates/story/story.php?storyId=124464928, accessed August 17, 2021.

13. Ricardo Arduengo, "Haiti Quake Creates Thousands of New Orphans." *NBC News*, January 2010. https://www.nbcnews.com/id/wbna34934553, accessed September 8, 2021.

14. Chantel Dooley. TAPS Research & Impact Assessment from Tragedy Assistance Program for Survivors (TAPS), through email on August 13, 2021.

CHAPTER 2

1. Thad, email interview, September 13, 2021.
2. Jessica, email interview, May 10, 2021.
3. Liz, email interview, August 30, 2021.
4. Travis, email interview, April 14, 2021.
5. Dani R., email interview, May 4, 2021.
6. Reaghan, email interview, July 7, 2021.
7. Sharon, email interview, September 15, 2021.
8. *Twister*. Action/adventure/thriller, 1996. 113 minutes.

CHAPTER 3

1. *27 Dresses*. Comedy/romance, 2008. 111 minutes.
2. Georgianne, email interview, April 9, 2021.
3. Jessica, email interview, May 10, 2021.
4. Chase, email interview, August 5, 2021.

CHAPTER 4

1. Liz, email interview, August 30, 2021.
2. Thad, email interview, September 13, 2021.
3. Dani R., email interview, May 4, 2021.
4. Reaghan, email interview, July 7, 2021.
5. Sharon, email interview, September 15, 2021.
6. Reaghan, email interview, July 7, 2021.

CHAPTER 5

1. Reaghan, email interview, July 7, 2021.
2. Travis, email interview, April 14, 2021.
3. Jessica, email interview, May 10, 2021.
4. Dani R., email interview, May 4, 2021.
5. Lola, email interview, January 21, 2021.

CHAPTER 6

1. Taylor, email interview, September 19, 2021.

CHAPTER 8

1. Dani R., email interview, May 4, 2021.

CHAPTER 9

1. Lola, email interview, January 21, 2021.
2. Thad, email interview, September 13, 2021.
3. Jessica, email interview, May 10, 2021.
4. Sharon, email interview, September 15, 2021.
5. Chase, email interview, August 5, 2021.
6. Georgianne, email interview, April 9, 2021.

7. Travis, email interview, April 14, 2021.
8. Dani R., email interview, May 4, 2021.

CHAPTER 10

1. Lola, email interview, January 21, 2021.
2. Thad, email interview, September 13, 2021.
3. Sharon, email interview, September 15, 2021.
4. Dani R., May 4, 2021.
5. Lola, email interview, January 21, 2021.
6. Jessica, email interview, May 10, 2021.
7. Travis, email interview, April 14, 2021.
8. Sharon, email interview, September 15, 2021.
9. Thad, email interview, September 13, 2021.
10. Lola, email interview, January 21, 2021.
11. Jessica, email interview, May 10, 2021.
12. Liz, email interview, August 30, 2021.
13. Debbie, email interview, April 9, 2021.
14. Lola, email interview, January 21, 2021.
15. Liz, email interview, August 30, 2021.

CHAPTER 11

1. Lola, email interview, January 21, 2021.
2. Jessica, email interview, May 10, 2021.
3. Liz, email interview, August 30, 2021.
4. Lola, email interview, January 21, 2021.
5. Liz, email interview, August 30, 2021.
6. Lola, email interview, January 21, 2021.
7. Thad, email interview, September 13, 2021.

CHAPTER 12

1. "Alan Rickman," *Biography.com*, https://www.biography.com/actor/alan-rickman, accessed January 29, 2021.

2. "Benicio Del Toro," *Biography.com*, https://www.biography.com/actor/benicio-del-toro, accessed January 28, 2021.

3. "Billy Crystal," *IMDb.com*, https://www.imdb.com/name/nm0000345/bio, accessed January 29, 2021.

4. "Cate Blanchett," *IMDb.com*, https://www.imdb.com/name/nm0000949/bio, accessed January 29, 2021.

5. "Freddie Prinze Jr.," *IMDb.com*, https://www.imdb.com/name/nm0000249/bio, accessed January 29, 2021.

6. "James Woods," *IMDb.com*, https://www.imdb.com/name/nm0000249/bio, accessed January 29, 2021.

7. "John Goodman," *Biography.com*, https://www.biography.com/actor/john-goodman, accessed January 29, 2021.

8. "Molly Shannon," *IMDb.com*, https://www.imdb.com/name/nm0788340/bio, accessed January 29, 2021.

9. "Rosie O'Donnell," *Biography.com*, https://www.biography.com/performer/rosie-odonnell, accessed January 26, 2021.

10. "Tim Allen," *IMDb.com*, https://www.imdb.com/name/nm0000741/bio, accessed January 29, 2021.

11. "Zoe Saldana," *Biography.com*, https://www.biography.com/actor/zoe-saldana, accessed January 29, 2021.

12. "Gabrielle Reece," *GabrielleReece.com*, https://www.gabriellereece.com/bio/, accessed January 29, 2021.

13. "Ronda Rousey," *Biography.com*, https://www.biography.com/athlete/ronda-rousey, accessed January 29, 2021.

14. Jess Belmosto, "Flames' Hamonic Offers Grieving Families a Shoulder to Lean On," *TheHockeyWriters.com*, March 17, 2020, https://thehockeywriters.com/flames-hamonic-d-partner-program/, accessed January 29, 2021.

15. "Amy Tan," *Biography.com*, https://www.biography.com/writer/amy-tan, accessed January 26, 2021.

16. "C. S. Lewis," *Biography.com*, https://www.biography.com/writer/cs-lewis, accessed January 26, 2021.

17. "Edgar Allan Poe," *Biography.com*, https://www.biography.com/writer/edgar-allan-poe, accessed January 26, 2021.

18. "J. R.R . Tolkien," *Biography.com*, https://www.biography.com/writer/jrr-tolkien, accessed January 26, 2021.

19. "Joseph Conrad," *Britannica.com*, https://www.britannica.com/biography/Joseph-Conrad, accessed January 26, 2021.

20. "Leo Tolstoy," *Biography.com*, https://www.biography.com/scholar/leo-tolstoy, accessed January 26, 2021.

21. "P. L. Travers," *Biography.com*, https://www.biography.com/writer/pl-travers, accessed January 26, 2021.

22. "Elizabeth Blackwell," *Biography.com*, https://www.biography.com/sci entist/elizabeth-blackwell, accessed January 28, 2021.

23. "Anne Sullivan," *Biography.com*, https://www.biography.com/activist/ anne-sullivan, accessed January 26, 2021.

24. "Karl Benz," *Biography.com*, https://www.biography.com/inventor/karl -benz, accessed January 26, 2021.

25. "William Boeing: The Story of a Visionary Aircraft Manufacturer," *DisciplesofFlight.com*, December 17, 2015, https://disciplesofflight.com/william -boeing/, accessed January 26, 2021.

26. "Irena Sendler," *Biography.com*, https://www.biography.com/activist/ irena-sendler, accessed January 28, 2021.

27. "Ruth Bader Ginsburg," *Biography.com*, https://www.biography.com/ law-figure/ruth-bader-ginsburg, accessed January 26, 2021.

28. "Sonia Sotomayor," *Biography.com*, https://www.biography.com/law -figure/sonia-sotomayor, accessed January 26, 2021.

29. "Elias Canetti," *Britannica.com*, https://www.britannica.com/biography/ Elias-Canetti, accessed January 28, 2021.

30. "Jean-Paul Sartre," *Britannica.com*, https://www.britannica.com/biogra phy/Jean-Paul-Sartre, accessed January 28, 2021.

31. "Linus Pauling Biography," *Encyclopedia of World Biography*, https:// www.notablebiographies.com/Ni-Pe/Pauling-Linus.html, accessed January 28, 2021.

32. "Mother Teresa," *Biography.com*, https://www.biography.com/religious -figure/mother-teresa, accessed January 20, 2021.

33. "Severo Ochoa," *Encyclopedia.com*, https://www.encyclopedia.com/peo ple/medicine/medicine-biographies/severo-ochoa, accessed January 29, 2021.

34. "Kawabata Yasunari," *Britannica.com*, https://www.britannica.com/bi ography/Kawabata-Yasunari, accessed January 28, 2021.

35. "Anderson Cooper," *Biography.com*, https://www.biography.com/me dia-figure/anderson-cooper, accessed January 26, 2021.

36. "Drew Carey," *Biography.com*, https://www.biography.com/performer/ drew-carey, accessed January 26, 2021.

CHAPTER 15

1. Liz, email interview, August 30, 2021.

2. Sharon, email interview, September 15, 2021.

3. Taylor, email interview, September 19, 2021.

4. Thad, email interview, September 13, 2021.

5. Chase, email interview, August 5, 2021.

6. Nicci, email interview, April 18, 2021.
7. Georgianne, email interview, April 9, 2021.
8. Travis, email interview, April 14, 2021.
9. Dani R., email interview, May 4, 2021.
10. Lola, email interview, January 21, 2021.
11. Reaghan, email interview, July 7, 2021.
12. Debbie, email interview, April 9, 2021.
13. Jessica, email interview, May 10, 2021.

Resources

GRIEF APP

https://healgrief.org/amf-app/

GRIEF CAMPS

Camp Erin/Eluna Network, https://elunanetwork.org/camps
-programs/camp-erin
Comfort Zone Camp, http://www.comfortzonecamp.org

JOURNALS

Deconstruction reconstruction journal, https://dougybookstore
.org/products/deconstruction-reconstruction-a-grief-journal
-for-teens
Healing Your Grieving Hearts for Teens Journal, https://www
.centerforloss.com/bookstore/The-Healing-Your-Grieving-Heart
-Journal-for-Teens/
Our House My Grief Journal for Teens, https://www.ourhouse
-grief.org/product/my-grief-journal-for-teens/

ORGANIZATIONS

American Hospice Foundation, https://americanhospice.org/ grieving-children/someone-you-love-has-died-a-book-for-griev ing-children/

Annie's Hope, http://annieshope.org/

Because Kids Grieve, https://becausekidsgrieve.org/

Billy's Place, https://billsplace.me/-1

COPS., https://www.concernsofpolicesurvivors.org/

Charlie's Guys, https://www.charliesguys.org/

Children of Fallen Police Officers Foundation, https://www.police officersfoundation.org/

Coalition to Support Grieving Students, https://grievingstudents .org/

Eluna Network, https://elunanetwork.org/

Empowering Her, https://www.empoweringher.org/about

Fallen Patriots, https://www.fallenpatriots.org/

Funeral Service Foundation, https://www.funeralservicefoundation .org/resources/youth-and-funerals/

Good Grief https://good-grief.org/

Heal Grief, https://healgrief.org/helping-children-cope-deal -with-grief/

Imagine, A Center for Coping with Loss, https://imaginenj.org/

Motherless Daughters, https://www.motherlessdaughters.com/

National Center for School Crisis and Bereavement, https://www .schoolcrisiscenter.org/

New Song Center for Grieving Children, https://www.hov.org/ our-care/grief-support/new-song-center-for-grieving-children/

Our House Grief Support Center, https://www.ourhouse-grief .org/children-and-teens/

Ryan's Place, https://ryansplace.org/

TAPS, https://www.taps.org/

The Austin Center for Grief & Loss, https://www.austingrief.org/ childrenservices

The Children's Room, https://childrensroom.org/resources/teen _grief_resources/

The Dougy Center, https://www.dougy.org/

The Family Lives On Foundation, https://www.familyliveson.org/
support-for-students-who-have-lost-a-parent-the-family-lives
-on-foundation/

The Garden: A Center for Grieving Children and Teens, https://
www.cooleydickinson.org/programs-services/vna-hospice/the
-garden/

The National Alliance for Children's Grief, https://childrengrieve
.org/

Valerie's House, https://valerieshouse.org/

Bibliography

"Alan Rickman," *Biography.com*, https://www.biography.com/actor/alan-rick
man, accessed January 29, 2021.

"Amy Tan," *Biography.com*, https://www.biography.com/writer/amy-tan, accessed January 26, 2021.

"Anderson Cooper," *Biography.com*, https://www.biography.com/media-fig
ure/anderson-cooper, accessed January 26, 2021.

"Anne Sullivan," *Biography.com*, https://www.biography.com/activist/anne
-sullivan, accessed January 26, 2021.

Arduengo, Ricardo. "Haiti Quake Creates Thousands of New Orphans."
January 2010, *NBC News*. https://www.nbcnews.com/id/wbna34934553,
accessed September 8, 2021.

Avert. "Children, HIV, and AIDS." https://www.avert.org/professionals/hiv
-social-issues/key-affected-populations/children, accessed August 17, 2021.

Belmosto, Jess "Flames' Hamonic Offers Grieving Families a Shoulder to Lean
On," *TheHockeyWriters.com*, March 17, 2020, https://thehockeywriters.com/
flames-hamonic-d-partner-program/, accessed January 29, 2021.

"Benicio del Toro," *Biography.com*, https://www.biography.com/actor/benicio-
del-toro, accessed January 28, 2021.

"Billy Crystal," *IMDb.com*, https://www.imdb.com/name/nm0000345/bio, accessed January 29, 2021.

"C.S. Lewis," *Biography.com*, https://www.biography.com/writer/cs-lewis, accessed January 26, 2021.

"Cate Blanchett," *IMDb.com*, https://www.imdb.com/name/nm0000949/bio,
accessed January 29, 2021.

Clifford, Rebecca. "Families after the Holocaust: Between the Archives and
Oral History." *Oral History* 46, no. 1 (2018): 42–54 https://www.jstor.org/
stable/44993455 accessed, August 17, 2021.

Dooley, Chantel. TAPS Research & Impact Assessment from TAPS, Tragedy
Assistance Program for Survivors, through email on August 13, 2021.

Drash, Wayne. "'Daddy's in Heaven': Rig Victims' Families Share Memories, Mementos." August 2010, *CNN.com*. http://www.cnn.com/2010/US/07/29/rig.victim.families/index.html, accessed August 17, 2021.

"Drew Carey," *Biography.com*, https://www.biography.com/performer/drew-carey, accessed January 26, 2021.

"Edgar Allan Poe, *Biography.com*, https://www.biography.com/writer/edgar-allan-poe, accessed January 26, 2021.

"Elias Canetti," *Britannica.com*, https://www.britannica.com/biography/Elias-Canetti, accessed January 28, 2021.

"Elizabeth Blackwell," *Biography.com*, https://www.biography.com/scientist/elizabeth-blackwell, accessed January 28, 2021.

Elliott, Debbie. "In Haiti, Quake's Orphans Long for a Home." March 9, 2010, *NPR*. https://www.npr.org/templates/story/story.php?storyId=124464928, accessed August 17, 2021.

"Freddie Prinze Jr.," *IMDb.com*, https://www.imdb.com/name/nm0000249/bio, accessed January 29, 2021.

"Gabrielle Reece," *GabrielleReece.com*, https://www.gabriellereece.com/bio/, accessed January 29, 2021.

"Households with Kids Who Lost Parents in Great East Japan Quake and Tsunami Face Poverty." *The Mainichi*, December 12, 2020. https://mainichi.jp/english/articles/20201212/p2a/00m/0na/016000c, accessed August 17, 2021.

"Irena Sendler," *Biography.com*, https://www.biography.com/activist/irena-sendler, accessed January 28, 2021.

"J.R.R. Tolkien," *Biography.com*, https://www.biography.com/writer/jrr-tolkien, accessed January 26, 2021.

"James Woods," *IMDb.com*, https://www.imdb.com/name/nm0000249/bio, accessed January 29, 2021.

"Jean-Paul Sartre," *Britannica.com*, https://www.britannica.com/biography/Jean-Paul-Sartre, accessed January 28, 2021.

"John Goodman," *Biography.com*, https://www.biography.com/actor/john-goodman, accessed January 29, 2021.

Johns Hopkins Medicine. "Children Who Lose a Parent to Suicide More Likely to Die the Same Way." April 21, 2010. https://www.hopkinsmedicine.org/news/media/releases/children_who_lose_a_parent_to_suicide_more_likely_to_die_the_same_way, accessed August 17, 2021.

"Joseph Conrad," *Britannica.com*, https://www.britannica.com/biography/Joseph-Conrad, accessed January 26, 2021.

"Karl Benz," *Biography.com*, https://www.biography.com/inventor/karl-benz, accessed January 26, 2021.

"Kawabata Yasunari," *Britannica.com*, https://www.britannica.com/biography/Kawabata-Yasunari, accessed January 28, 2021.

"Leo Tolstoy," *Biography.com*, https://www.biography.com/scholar/leo-tolstoy, accessed January 26, 2021.

Linenthal, Edward Tabor. "Oklahoma City Bombing." In Oklahoma Historical Society, *The Encyclopedia of Oklahoma History and Culture*. https://www.okhistory.org/publications/enc/entry.php?entry=OK026, accessed August 17, 2021.

"Linus Pauling Biography," *Encyclopedia of World Biography*, https://www.notablebiographies.com/Ni-Pe/Pauling-Linus.html, accessed January 28, 2021.

"Molly Shannon," *IMDb.com*, https://www.imdb.com/name/nm0788340/bio, accessed January 29, 2021.

"Mother Teresa," *Biography.com*, https://www.biography.com/religious-figure/mother-teresa, accessed January 20, 2021.

Motich, Elizabeth. "Orphans of the Front in World War I." Villanova University Remembering WWI project website. https://rememberingwwi.villanova.edu/orphans/, accessed August 17, 2021.

National Center for Biotechnology Information and US National Library of Medicine. "Improving emotional health and self-esteem of Malaysian adolescents living in orphanages through Life Skills Education program: A multi-centre randomized control trial." *NCBI* website, December 26, 2019. https://www.ncbi.nlm.nih.gov/pmc/articles/PMC6932807/, accessed August 17, 2021.

"Ochoa, Severo," *Encyclopedia.com*, https://www.encyclopedia.com/people/medicine/medicine-biographies/severo-ochoa, accessed January 29, 2021.

"P. L. Travers," *Biography.com*, https://www.biography.com/writer/pl-travers, accessed January 26, 2021.

Preidt, Robert. "1.5 Million Kids Worldwide Lost Parent or Other Caregiver to COVID-19." July 2021, *US NEWS*. https://www.usnews.com/news/health-news/articles/2021-07-21/15-million-kids-worldwide-lost-parent-or-other-caregiver-to-covid-19, accessed August 17, 2021.

"Ronda Rousey," *Biography.com*, https://www.biography.com/athlete/ronda-rousey, accessed January 29, 2021.

"Rosie O'Donnell," *Biography.com*, https://www.biography.com/performer/rosie-odonnell, accessed January 26, 2021.

"Ruth Bader Ginsburg," *Biography.com*, https://www.biography.com/law-figure/ruth-bader-ginsburg, accessed January 26, 2021.

"Sonia Sotomayor," *Biography.com*, https://www.biography.com/law-figure/sonia-sotomayor, accessed January 26, 2021.

"Tim Allen," *IMDb.com*, https://www.imdb.com/name/nm0000741/bio, accessed January 29, 2021.

United for the Fallen. "Mission Statement." https://theunitedforthefallen.com/, accessed August 17, 2021.

Uwiringiyimana, Clement. "Now Grown Up: The Rwandan Genocide Orphans Who Found a Bigger Family." April 4, 2019. *Reuters.* https://www.reuters.com/article/us-rwanda-genocide-families-idUSKCN1RG1D5, accessed August 17, 2021.

"Widows and Orphans." Encyclopedia.com https://www.encyclopedia.com/defense/energy-government-and-defense-magazines/widows-and-orphans, accessed August 17, 2021.

"William Boeing: The Story of a Visionary Aircraft Manufacturer," *Disciplesof-Flight.com,* December 17, 2015, https://disciplesofflight.com/william-boeing/, accessed January 26, 2021.

Winterman, Denise. "Children of the Great War." *BBC News* Magazine. http://news.bbc.co.uk/2/hi/uk_news/magazine/7082625.stm, accessed August 17, 2021.

"Zoe Saldana," *Biography.com,* https://www.biography.com/actor/zoe-saldana, accessed January 29, 2021.

Index

About the Author

Like the readers of this book, **Michelle Shreeve** lost her mother young when she was only nine years old. She holds two master's degrees in English and creative writing and two undergraduate degrees in psychology. She wrote her master's degree thesis project on how bibliotherapy and writing therapy with the use of auto-ethnography can help children, teenagers, and young adults navigate their grief from parental death at a young age to use as a therapeutic coping mechanism. Shreeve has been a published local and national freelance writer since 2008, having often written about the subject of parental death at a young age. She also has more than 10 years of experience in the education and library field. This is Shreeve's second nonfiction book traditionally published regarding the subject of parental death at a young age. Her first book, *Parental Death: The Ultimate Teen Guide* was a part of Rowman & Littlefield's It Happened to Me series published in 2018. Her personal story of parental death at a young age was featured on a local radio show and was featured nationally in *Korean Guideposts* magazine. Shreeve's freelance work has been published in a variety of outlets such as newspapers, magazines, blogs, and websites such as *Publisher's Weekly, Ahwatukee Foothills Newspaper, Life Aspire,* Southern New Hampshire University, *East Valley Tribune, Peoria Times, Gilbert Sun News,* Southern New Hampshire University *Impact magazine, West Valley Magazine,* Mindfulness and Grief Institute, *Examiner.com,* and more. She also has a background in reviewing books and movies, which has especially come in handy while writing this book because Shreeve finds that using book and movie references (bibliotherapy and movie therapy) can be helpful relatable supplementary coping tools that children, teens, and young adults can use while trying to gain personal insight into the loss of their parent at a young age. Shreeve and her husband Chris also make personalized glass etchings, vinyl decals, stickers, t-shirts, sticker books, ornaments, and more for children, teens, young adults, and adults who are trying to preserve the memory of their late parent as well as help cope with their grief, through their *Okay Custom Creations* side business. Shreeve can be reached at parentaldeath@gmail.com.